LAW SCHOOL 2.0

Legal Education for a Digital Age

LAW SCHOOL 2.0

Legal Education for a Digital Age

DAVID I. C. THOMSON

LP Professor and Director
Lawyering Process Program
University of Denver
Sturm College of Law

 LexisNexis®

Library of Congress Cataloging-in-Publication Data

Thomson., David I. C.
   Law school 2.0 / David I.C. Thomson.
       p. cm.
   Includes index.
   ISBN 978-1-4224-2700-2 (softbound)
   1. Law—Study and teaching. 2. Law—Computer-assisted instruction. 3. Web 2.0.
I. Title.
   K100.T48 2008
   340.071′1—dc22

                                       2008047381

This publication is designed to provide accurate and authoritative information in regard to the subject matter covered. It is sold with the understanding that the publisher is not engaged in rendering legal, accounting, or other professional services. If legal advice or other expert assistance is required, the services of a competent professional should be sought.

NOTE TO USERS
To ensure that you are using the latest materials available in this area, please be sure to periodically check the LexisNexis Law School web site for downloadable updates and supplements at www.lexisnexis.com/lawschool.

Editorial Offices
744 Broad Street, Newark, NJ 07102 (973) 820-2000
201 Mission St., San Francisco, CA 94105-1831 (415) 908-3200
www.lexisnexis.com

MATTHEW◆BENDER

(2009—Pub.3288)

DEDICATION

To my esteemed colleague Fred Cheever,
who saw this book in my work
well before I did.

INTRODUCTION

Legal education is at a crossroads. As today's media-saturated students enter law school, they find themselves thrust into old style lecture-oriented, casebook modes of instruction, much of which is over 100 years old. Over those years legal education has resisted many studies recommending change, most recently those from the Carnegie Foundation for the Advancement of Teaching and the Clinical Legal Education Association. Meanwhile the cost of legal education has skyrocketed, many law students graduate with crushing debt they have difficulty paying back, and at the same time find that their training has left them ill-equipped to practice in an ever-changing global marketplace. These factors are likely to worsen in the next few years, setting up a perfect storm out of which can finally come significant change.

But legal education has successfully resisted systemic change for many years. Given this dubious track record, the only way significant change can reasonably be predicted is if something is different this time.   Fortunately, there is something different this time: the ubiquity of technology. Since the last report recommending change in legal education (in 1992), the Internet has achieved massive growth. A generation of students has grown up with the sophisticated and pervasive use of technology in nearly every facet of their lives. Computers are how today's law students communicate and learn. Fortunately, this same technology presents legal educators with a golden opportunity to reach students unlike any that have been available before.

This book will describe how this profound generational change both should and will transform the face of legal education as we know it today. It will cover the new ways our students learn, the pedagogical shifts that will occur inside and outside the classroom, a new breed of hybrid textbooks that will appear, and effective new methods of active, interactive and hypertextual learning. Most important, this book will describe simple ways in which teachers can harness this shift to better prepare law students of today for the practice of law tomorrow.

There is always, of course, resistance to change and recently much gnashing of teeth has been going on in the legal academy. Nearly everyone agrees that change is called for, but many feel real progress is unlikely — the costs are too high, law schools suffer from terminal inertia, law faculties are not set up to teach in these new ways, and so on. Meanwhile, we are in a period when quite a few law schools have recently chosen to install at least one fairly radical reform in their curricula. One has changed its third year of law school to a completely clinical model. Another has put more focus on the administrative state in its first year program. The problem with these reforms is that they lack an organizing principle — other than a general conception of "being more relevant to practice." The faculties have approved these changes, but they seem to have little in the way of a precise reason why. Such partial curricular reforms bring to mind the image of electrode paddles jolting a heart attack patient in the emergency room. The paddles may keep the patient from dying that day, but the body is still pretty sick.

We cannot fault some faculty members' skepticism that these reforms will eventually fail or die out — others certainly have before. Professor Martha Minow at Harvard Law School chaired a reform committee that succeeded in making some significant changes in Harvard's curriculum. Speaking at a 2008 conference, she summed up the resistances to change that she faced in her committee's work: "You get responses from faculty members that cover the waterfront. They will either say: 'We have tried that before.' Or they will say: 'We have never tried that before.'"[1]

The title of this book refers to Web 2.0, a term that encompasses the second generation of web technologies which support user participation and content creation. While the term "<fill in the blank>2.0" has come to generically mean something is new and changed from what came before, by using the title "Law School 2.0" I mean not just to suggest that legal education is changing, but also that forces in the technological realm — of which Web 2.0 plays a significant part — will be a catalyst for this change. In short, this book posits that technology will both force change and can *facilitate* and *lubricate* its coming to legal education. At least I believe it can — if legal educators embrace it, and are willing to learn how to leverage it for this purpose. It seems likely that we must, because the forces pushing against the historical resistances to change will be too strong to resist.

Responsibility for the success of Law School 2.0 falls on legal educators who will need to lead our schools into a better and more effective future. The subject of this book — change in legal education — is of critical importance well beyond the ivy-clad walls of law schools. The law serves a central function in our participatory democracy and without lawyers who are fully capable of functioning in the legal profession of tomorrow our country will quickly find itself in trouble. Law school faculties broadly understand and agree that if we fail to properly prepare attorneys for practice then we are not properly fulfilling our mission.

A growing body of research indicates that we may not only be failing to fulfill this mission, but also may actually be causing harm to our students. This research suggests that the inhumanity and disconnection of much of today's typical legal educational process can create lawyers who are ill-equipped to handle the emotional stresses of practice, or who may be destined to join the vast ranks of lawyers dissatisfied with their work. Extraordinary numbers of attorneys are

---

[1] Plenary Session; American Association of Law Schools Annual Meeting, Rethinking Legal Education for the 21st Century, Jan. 4, 2008.

clinically depressed, far more than in any other profession. That troubling fact not only casts doubt on law as a profession, but also reflects poorly on the quality and design of legal education.

This book seeks to bring all of this together: the changes in our students, in technology, and in the needs of the profession. It envisions a new sort of law school that will be organized around a different teaching model, one that is more supportive of its students and embraces the pedagogical gifts that technology has brought and will continue to bring us. It is not just focused on preparing students for practice, but rather on preparing them for the practice of the future.

Like all authors, I write this book from my own point of view, formed by my own experience. Some readers may disagree with what I say here, and some of them may have had more experience than I do with law school teaching. I practiced law for 20 years before switching to full-time teaching. My practice experience was in litigation, first at a large New York City law firm, then as an environmental enforcement trial attorney at the U.S. Department of Justice. I then worked as an attorney for Price Waterhouse and was part of a consulting group that helped law firms with their automation requirements. After that I moved to a Denver law firm for three years, then guided an internet business, and then joined a small litigation firm with a partner and three associates.

More than 15 years ago, the University of Denver law school hired me as an adjunct professor to teach sections of the newly formed "Lawyering Process" course, which I did for six years while also practicing law and serving on the Legal Education and Admissions Committee of the Colorado Bar Association. This year marks my 13th year teaching in a law school, seven of which were while serving as an adjunct professor. As a result of my journey, I bring my diverse experience to this effort both in law practice in large law firms, small law firms, in government service, corporate law offices and business, as well as in law teaching. In all my years of practice and teaching I have been on the front lines as a witness of and an advocate for the role technology increasingly plays in both fields.

This combination of experience and background helped to peel the scales off my eyes when I joined the full-time faculty at the University of Denver in 2003. That first year back, it seemed to me like a whole new ball game, certainly different from when I had gone to law school 20 years before, and even substantially different from when I had earlier taught essentially the same course at the same school as an adjunct professor. That first year teaching full-time I felt as though I was teaching a new sort of student. Something about them had changed significantly. I became engaged in learning about the nature of this change and what it meant for my own law teaching. Over the past five years, I have tested many of the technologies described in this book, including Wikis, Clickers and Podcasting, and over the last four years I have taught two different law courses online.

Much has been already been written about the "Millennial" generation — those born after 1982 who began to reach college around the year 2000—but two things about them are obvious to everyone: they are saturated by electronic media and totally comfortable with computers and other forms of the latest technology. It is also obvious that the law practice they go into will be wired into this technology as never before. It seemed to me beyond obvious that these simple truths must affect how we teach them. The interesting question, and discussion, is found in sorting that out. This book comes out of my conviction that we can harness technology to reach this generation more effectively than we do now. Simply put, I feel strongly that we must be in the business of preparing our students *for their future, not our past.*

But this is intended to be neither a futuristic romp nor a "baby-out-with-the-bathwater" book. There are plenty of things about legal education that work well and should not be changed. In many ways a time traveling law professor from today would recognize the law school of the future, but there is an important conversation that we need to have now: about how technology can facilitate the changes that many agree need to be made but are hard to make and harder to sustain. In my view it is imperative that we have this conversation. If we continue the way we have been going, resisting change — or simply engaging in a series of curricular experiments — over time our work will become less relevant to our students.

And that would be a tragedy not just for us and not just for our students, but also for the world we are preparing them to engage.

So this book comes out of many years of practice experience, broad experience with the uses of technology to support legal practice and learning, and familiarity with the challenges of legal education. While I feel this mixture of experience gives me something to say about the future of legal education, I offer my thoughts not as an answer but simply in the hope that they will encourage a constructive discussion of these complex questions. And while there is some description here of my vision of what legal education will look like one day, I offer it with respect for the fact that, in the words of the great physicist Niels Bohr, "Prediction is very difficult, especially of the future."

Further information about the issues and themes presented in this book, can be found at:
http://www.lawschool2.com

Note: The graphics at the beginning of each chapter in this book are called "wordles." Wordles are a form of tag cloud, which represent word or topic popularity. The tag clouds at the beginning of each chapter indicate the relative frequency of the words that appear in the chapter that follows them.

Wordles are a form of visualization of large data sets, a topic that is described in Chapters 4 and 6. More information about wordles and other forms of visualizations can be found at www.wordle.com.

ACKNOWLEDGMENTS

As with any such effort, there are many who have supported it and I want to offer them my thanks and gratitude. I must first acknowledge the assistance and perspective provided by the nearly 500 students over the last five years whom I have had the honor to teach in at least one of five different courses. Among those students, I must especially acknowledge the assistance of my Teaching Assistants for Technology, Katy Micka (who originated the role), and her worthy successor, Jeff Sparhawk. Katy and Jeff were exceedingly savvy technology users in their law studies, and they provided me with helpful and detailed information about student use of technology at our law school and beyond. In addition, they helped me to keep track of the rapid developments in the area by peppering me with links to relevant web sites, and by sending me myriad articles and analyses of pedagogical technology. But perhaps most of all, Katy and Jeff supported this effort by simply affirming for me that I was — at least roughly — on the right track. In most cases, validation by peers is what teachers and scholars seek, and I am no exception to that rule. But in the case of the subject of this book, validation by such knowledgeable and articulate students has also been invaluable. For all of their work and support, I give them my deep gratitude.

I also want to acknowledge those colleagues in the law school professorate who are engaged in similar and related questions as those addressed here. Among those, I especially want to thank Diana Donohoe (Georgetown), Ian Gallacher (Syracuse), Tracy McGaugh (Tuoro), Michael Schwartz (Washburn), Don Smith (Denver), and Cliff Zimmerman (Northwestern). I have discussed many of these topics on numerous occasions over the years with these colleagues, and have always come away enriched by our conversations.

A portion of this work and thinking was shaped and formed at the Legal Writing Institute's Writer's Workshop, at Chautauqua in Boulder, Colorado in June, 2007. I was honored to work with and learn from the Workshop's leaders:

Steve Johansen (Lewis & Clark), Chris Rideout (Seattle), Linda Edwards (Mercer), and particularly my group's leader: Jill Ramsfield (Hawaii). In leading our small group, Jill was tremendously helpful in validating the work as needing more treatment than a short article or two.

Some of this work was supported by a grant from the Association of Legal Writing Directors, which I was awarded in 2005. That grant supported the early work in online pedagogy, which is described in Chapter 7. I also acknowledge the support of the University of Denver's Center for Teaching and Learning, which provided a T&L Grant in 2004 that lead to my study of collaborative learning in the first year of law school. Assisting me in that work was Dr. Sheila Summers-Thompson, who was then Assistant Provost for Institutional Research and Assessment at DU. Sheila is now the Director of Student Learning and Outcomes Assessment at Metro State College in Denver, but over the last several years she has been a tremendous sounding board for much of this work and thought.

I acknowledge with gratitude the research support provided by Beto Juárez, Dean of the University of Denver's Sturm College of Law, over the summers of 2007 and 2008. This support allowed me to reduce (in 2007) and eliminate (in 2008) my summer teaching load, and without that teaching relief, I could not have found the time to complete this work. I also offer my gratitude and thanks to Associate Dean Penny Bryan, who has been unfailingly supportive of my work over the years. And I am indebted to my colleagues on the DU law faculty Professors Arthur Best and Eli Wald for reading and commenting on an earlier version of the manuscript.

A special thanks to Diane Burkhardt, Faculty Research Librarian at the Westminster Law Library at the University of Denver. Over the last several years, Diane has kept up to date on my research interests, and regularly sent me items that contributed to my understanding of these issues. In addition, during the writing of the book, she was tireless in tracking down sources, and was unfailingly encouraging throughout. I am similarly indebted to my student research assistants over the last two years, Kendra Beckwith Grobelny, Chad Grell, and Eileen Joy. I also thank my administrative assistants,

Jessica Neumann and Emily Jodock, for cheerfully accomplishing myriad tasks in support of this effort.

Many thanks also are due to the folks at LexisNexis, among them Scott Koorndyk, Leslie Levin, Sean Caldwell, Kelli Eagle, and my editor Mike Mintz. All have supported this work in many ways, and I am grateful to them.

Finally, a few personal notes: a note of thanks to my late mother, Frances Coombs Thomson, from whom I learned so much about writing. And also to my father, David S. Thomson, who continues to be unfailingly encouraging about my writing efforts and who offered helpful editing suggestions on this one. I must also express a heartfelt thank you to my mother and father-in-law, Dan and Flora Russel, who have lent their "Casita" in Santa Fe to me for weeks at a time over the last few years. The time away has been invaluable; having a place to do nothing but read, think, and write has been essential — this book would not exist without those periods of focused effort. Also, a note of thanks to my sister-in-law Marquita Russel, who provided much hospitality during my trips to Santa Fe.

This book is dedicated to Professor Federico Cheever at the University of Denver. As my mentor, colleague, and friend, it was Fred who recognized that I should write about this work, and further, that it belonged in book form. It was Fred who believed it could be done, Fred who talked me through large portions of it, and Fred who read through early drafts and offered suggestions. In short, you would not be reading this book but for Fred, and I am forever in his debt.

Lastly, I express my heartfelt gratitude to my wife Kathy, and my daughters Angelina and Sarah-Jane. Anyone with a family who attempts such an effort inevitably nibbles at the already limited time available to spend with their spouse and children, and this has been no exception. At times, I have not only nibbled, I have needed large chunks of time, especially the weeks spent in Santa Fe. I am profoundly grateful for their love and support.

TABLE OF CONTENTS

Chapter 1

THE LAW STUDENTS OF TODAY AND TOMORROW

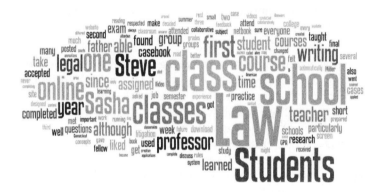

As a way of introducing some of the themes and concepts in this book, I have created two fictional law students; in this chapter their fictionalized law school experiences are described. The first is Steve Miller, who attended a top-25 law school in the recent past. He is modeled after many students a lot of us went to school with and others we have seen in our classes. Indeed, Steve represents a fairly typical law student experience even today. The second fictional student is Sasha Lujan, who attends law school approximately 10–15 years from now, in the future contemplated and described in this book. She represents what I hope will be a typical law school experience in the future when "Law School 2.0" will be the norm.

Steve

Steven Miller went to an Ivy-league college, but did not join a fraternity or play sports. He had a strong creative streak and at first majored in English and creative writing. He changed his major to economics because his uncle told him he would never make any money as a writer, but he was not sure what to do with his degree as his senior year approached. He knew a number of fellow students who were applying for jobs in the financial industry, but that did not sound very interesting, and he felt he did not have sufficient connections to land one of those jobs. His father was an attorney in a small firm in Connecticut, and although he seemed to like it well enough, he never gave Steve the impression that he loved practicing law. Nevertheless, Steve applied to law school primarily because he was not sure what he wanted to do after college. He only applied to a few top-25 schools, was accepted by two of them, and finally decided to attend his father's alma mater. His father agreed to pay half of his tuition.

Steve found law school boring and difficult. The large lecture classes (the "casebook" courses) were taught primarily by older professors who had taught the same courses for many years. They typically used a modified Socratic method of teaching, with the students reading appellate cases in the subject before class, and the teacher calling on students randomly to question them about the cases that had been assigned. One particular teacher seemed to take pleasure in humiliating students and everyone lived in fear of him. Although the students respected this teacher, and nearly always completed the assigned reading, they hated the class and the way the teacher operated. In other classes, the student to be called upon was assigned ahead of time. In this class the students felt less dread, but unless they were the one assigned for the day they sometimes failed to do all their assigned reading. They liked this teacher better but respected her less.

Steve's favorite class was in legal writing and research. This was the class that made him feel most like a lawyer and he felt he was asked to do things that he had seen his father do. Unfortunately, the course was taught by an adjunct professor who practiced full time and Steve eventually got discouraged about a lack of sufficient feedback. He liked the teacher very much, and respected her the most of all of his teachers, but felt he had not gained a solid grasp of the difficult subject at the end of the first year. Everyone told him this was the most important class he would take in law school, but the school only gave the course 2 credits per semester, and by having it taught by adjuncts clearly sent a message that it was not important. After a while it became obvious to Steve that his fellow students were instead focusing on their casebook courses since their grades in these courses would carry the most weight in their GPA.

At the end of the semester, all the first year casebook courses ended with a final exam, which counted for the entire grade. This created a great deal of stress for Steve since he was not especially adept at this form of assessment and had had little practice with it in college. Because his class notes were spotty and unclear, he purchased commercially-available outlines for each of his courses and studied from those. He managed to get through the exam period, although during one exam he got sick and was not able to complete it. He managed to get a grade of "B" in each of his classes except the one that he was not able to complete; he got a C- in that one.

In the first year casebook courses, most students paid attention only intermittently. This became particularly pronounced in the upper level classes after the first year. During his second year Steve went to most of his classes but not all, and he only completed the reading occasionally. He had learned that he could cram from the commercial outlines, and do sufficiently well so that he did not need to pay a great deal of attention in class. He continued to get grades in the B range.

In the summer between his second and third years, Steve tried to get a job at a law firm or government office, but was unsuccessful. His father offered him a job working with him in his office in Connecticut, and Steve accepted it that so he did not have to keep looking for something else. On the second day of the job, his father asked him to draft a set of answers to interrogatories in a litigation he was handling. Although Steve vaguely remembered the subject coming up in civil procedure during the first year, he did not know what an interrogatory was, and stayed up late that night so he could figure out what to do without his father knowing. He did a terrible job and his father rewrote the drafts completely. After that, for the rest of the summer, he only gave his son research projects.

By third year, Steve was bored by the remaining required courses and nearly stopped going to class altogether. He tried but was unable to get accepted into one of the legal clinics. He did take two seminars with engaging professors and he liked those classes more. He also liked that he was able to write papers instead of taking final exams in those classes, and he did better as a result.

After gradua-
tion, Steve took a
job working for his
father. While he
took some satisfac-
tion in his work, he
was mostly bored
with it. He often
wondered if he had
made the right de-
cision in going to
law school.

Sasha

When she was in college, Sasha Lujan became interested in social work. She had worked for a summer on an Native American reservation in New Mexico and while there she had learned about child and family concerns among the tribes, and the legal issues surrounding them. That lead her to think she might want to go to law school but she wasn't sure. She found an online site that contained short videos of lawyers in various types of practice talking about their work and she found that quite interesting.

When it came time to apply, she conducted research on eleven different law schools completely online. She joined a chat group of other prospective students and for several evenings they met online to discuss what they had learned about the schools they were interested in. Although at first Sasha placed great weight on the law school ranking in a national magazine, after joining several chat groups with other prospective law students, and talking to attorneys online and in the area, she realized that the magazine's ranking was not important. She decided to apply to three law schools and completed and submitted her applications online as well. She was notified of her acceptances via e-mail. She was in contact with Native American law students at one of the schools and they encouraged her to go there since it had an excellent program in that area of law. She decided to attend that school, a small, private law school in a major western city.

As she prepared to attend that school, she found a group of other accepted students online on Facebook. She corresponded with several of them and learned some of their faces from their posted pictures. She obtained a sublet apartment through one of the online friendships she formed. When she and her new friends saw each other at orientation, they already knew each other and soon formed online study groups. During the course of the semester, she got together with her study groups both online and in a study room at the law school. They found they still needed to meet face to face on occasion to discuss what they were learning.

As Sasha settled into law school, she attended her first classes, which were designed so that the students could become familiar with the technical aspects of the courses they were assigned. There was no need to go to the bookstore since all of their texts were in digital format. Sasha had paid for and downloaded all of her texts several weeks before school started. After the first week of school, the classes only met in person once every other week.

In the first two weeks of class, students worked collaboratively and with the professor to determine the content and sequence of the syllabus. Once that was resolved, students logged on to the course website to work with much of the content of the course.

In the online environment, the students were able to view videos of their professor explaining certain key concepts. They participated in group discussion with the professor and fellow students. And they completed short writing assignments, submitting them to the professor's teaching assistant for review and feedback. The students also collaboratively prepared a study outline for the course in a wiki, an online site that supported collaborative writing.

Sasha's semi-weekly in person classes were designed to encourage discussion of key legal precedents and were not in that way much different from traditional casebook classes. But now the professor had sophisticated technology that she could bring to bear to make the classroom more interactive for Sasha and her classmates. The old chalkboards and whiteboards had been replaced with three screens. The professor had a netbook designed to access net-based applications, a multi-touch screen, and an embedded student response system, each of which was running on a different screen. During class time the professor could interact with animations and diagrams on her netbook, or on the multi-touch screen that everyone could see, a running capture of which was automatically posted to the course website at the conclusion of class.

As the teacher asked questions of the class, each student was able to respond through software running on their cell phones, which tabulated responses and posted them automatically to the gradebook on the course website immediately after class. In most classes, instead of projecting her own netbook, the teacher used the third screen to project the netbook of a student volunteer, who might be the designated scribe for the class, or might be conducting research online to supplement the class, or both. Video clips were often used by the professor to illustrate points being made in class, and podcasts of each class were available for download so Sasha could listen to them on her ride home.

Sasha particularly liked the online textbook for the course. Although it had material that simply needed to be read, Sasha could easily download those to various media. While some of her friends liked to download them to their iPods through a text-to-speech program, Sasha preferred to download them to her Kindle eReader. But the best parts of the book were the interactive ones, which were available online. She was able to make legal concepts come alive through animations she could interact with, and the problem sets all included videos of a client being interviewed by the senior lawyer, and websites, hyperlinked documents, and legal research case files that had been partially completed. She could access these from her desktop machine, her electronic tablet, or her Internet-enabled cell phone. All three remained wirelessly in sync with each other at all times.

Sasha's legal writing class was taught by a full-time member of the faculty, a particularly dedicated teacher, who answered e-mails promptly and personally met with every student several times each semester to review their writing with them. In that course, after a period of instruction of varying length, the remainder of Sasha's time was spent working with her classmates in small collaborative groups. Since they all had tablet computers, group members were able to edit the examples the teacher had posted to a wiki site, and after the collaborative exercise, the teacher was able to project each group's revised writing on one of the classroom screens for everyone to see and discuss.

In the casebook courses, there were usually mid-term examinations with feedback from the professor and final exams. But the finals were focused on using doctrinal law in practice, and were a mix of multiple-choice, short answer and essay questions. It also included a web site and short video clip to provide the factual background for one of the exam questions. Sasha did not do well in the multiple-choice segments, but she was better at the short answers and essay questions, and she found the video question to be particularly engaging and life-like. She averaged B+ in her exams, and received an A- in her writing class.

In her second year of law school, Sasha was accepted into the juvenile law clinic and took one required casebook course, but the rest of her classes were "practicum" in form. That is, although the students read cases and learned legal rules, it was all accomplished within the context of learning real legal skills for practice. In her Discovery class, she not only learned what an interrogatory is, but also learned the rules that govern them as well as cases interpreting those rules, and, most particularly, how to write them and answer them in the context of a litigation. She was assigned an opposing counsel from the class, and Sasha and her classmate exchanged discovery documents in the litigation as they were learning about them in class. They used the same eFiling system that is currently used by the state and federal courts in her law school's jurisdiction. This system automatically e-mailed her opposing counsel a copy of her filing and simultaneously filed a copy with the "Court" — in this case, her professor. This sort of practicum course helped her not only to be ready for the realities and practicalities of the practice of law, but because there was so much writing involved, it also helped to improve her writing skills.

In her third year, two of Sasha's courses met only once a week and she spent the remainder of class time working online through a problem in a multi-player virtual world. In this "mock up" of an entire town, realistic legal problems cropped up, and there were numerous clients and characters whom she needed to interview to learn about the problems. Her professors guided the work each student was doing in the virtual town and provided feedback and suggestions as the semester went along.

After graduation, Sasha started her legal career with an environmental public interest group and was assigned to take over a substantial part of their pending litigation case load. Largely because of the nature and quality of her experiences in law school, she was fully prepared to take on these cases and represent the group in both state and federal courts around the region.

These hypothetical student sketches are intended, of course, to show how the curricula and teaching methods of the future will make legal education more effective, more interesting, more engaging, and more participatory than it has been in the past and remains in large measure today. And also how these fresh approaches will deliver a better and happier end product — a lawyer fully ready to contribute to the profession, and to be truly interested in it. The main topic of this book is very simply how we get — despite many obstacles — from here to there, from now to then.

Chapter 2

THE PERFECT STORM

While the opposition to change in legal education is strong[2], clouds are forming on the horizon and the winds of the coming storm will be very powerful. Like most such storms, this one will be powerful because so many different forces are coming together at the same time. Similar winds have blown through many media sectors already and — borrowing the title of a notable movie — have come to be called the "Perfect Storm." I use this term, now tired, with some trepidation. But because it expresses the idea that several strong forces, some of which have not previously existed, are heading for each other and growing, and that the result will be something that we have not seen before, it is an apt phrase. Long-brewing dissatisfaction with law school programs and profound alterations in legal practice will combine with a new and different generation of students leveraging advances in web technology to produce changes in

---

[2] *See* Ch. 5, The Criticisms of Legal Education.

legal education of a sort that we have never seen before. Of course the "Perfect Storm" metaphor breaks down here because real weather phenomena are short lived and much of this storm will take years to blow through law schools. But this is good because it gives us time to prepare for the changes to come. If we prepare well enough, it will result in a better future — for law schools certainly, but especially for our students and, eventually, the legal profession as a whole.

The Web

The first iteration of the web — which some of us remember was originally called the World Wide Web (and is why we still type "www" before each web site we seek) — began as a list of independent silos of information, each created by the individual who posted them. As an example, in the mid-1990s a Bob Dylan enthusiast posted a discography of the enigmatic rock star's work on a page on the web and, over time, many other pages linked to it. The term "web" refers to these linkages, and the concept of the user's ability to link across pages from one information source to another was given the term "hypertext." (It is from hypertext that we get the "http" that precedes web addresses. It stands for "hypertext transfer protocol.") Hypertext has done many things for all of us, but most importantly for the subject of this book, it has put in the hands of students the ability to control the path of their learning.

As these original concepts of the web were first devised, other Bob Dylan enthusiasts could link and click around the web and learn about their hero, but they could not do anything to the discography page — it was fully under the control of its author and owner. This early version of the web has been called "Web 1.0."

The term Web 2.0 is not particularly new; it came from a conference by the same title in 2004. The subject of the conference was the emerging technologies that were largely designed to allow users to interact with the information they found — to add to it, respond to it, and offer their own variations on the information. It is this development that has taken the Internet from its origins as a research source to the interactive, community building, participatory place that we know it to be today. In the web we know now, we do not just go to Amazon.com to research a new book or product, we also go to learn what others think of it in the reviews they have posted. We do not just visit a blog to hear what the blog's author thinks about Bob Dylan's music, we go to see what other people think as well, and to add our own thoughts about the subject.

Perhaps the best known example of Web 2.0 is Wikipedia, the online encyclopedia founded in 2001. Wikipedia was written in web software that was new at the time called a wiki (the Hawaiian word for "fast"). A wiki is designed to support collaborative writing. Wikipedia was to be an online encyclopedia written by — well, by everyone who wanted to contribute. It sounded like a preposterous idea at the time. The notion that everyone and anyone could write an encyclopedia together ran counter to our conception of an encyclopedia as something written by experts and scholars. But although there have been bumps along the way, Wikipedia is a massive success story of the Web 2.0 world. As of this writing, it contains more than 10 million articles in 250 languages. Every day hundreds of thousands of volunteers all over the world make edits and contributions to the encyclopedia.[3]

Wikipedia is only one example of Web 2.0, however. While there remain many information-only sites on the web, most new web sites offer the user an opportunity to interact with the information they contain. Most have open blog features, seek and publish user feedback, and many are simply designed, as Wikipedia is, to be communal sites largely created and driven by their users.

The important thing about Web 2.0 for legal education is that it has been, and will be, a fixture for most students entering law school. Students who are currently in high school and college live in a world where it is widely assumed that they can create, contribute, and generally interact with what they are learning. Increasingly they have been encouraged by their teachers to learn in this way.

---

[3] *See* Wikipeida, *About*, http://en.wikipedia.org/wiki/Wikipedia:About (last visited Sep. 13, 2008); *see also* Leslie Brooks Suzukamo, *Wikipedia wins over Web users*, ST. PAUL PIONEER PRESS, April 24, 2007, at C1.

The Millennial Generation

The generation that followed Generation X, sometimes called "Generation Y" or the "Net Generation," consists of those people born between 1982 and 2001. Given this timing, members of this generation started attending law school in 2004, and will be with us for the next 15 to 20 years.

It is a commonplace that members of the Millennial Generation are media saturated and technology savvy. While that may not be entirely true of all members of this generation — there remain concerns about a digital divide — it is overwhelmingly true of those students who are likely to go to law school. Common characteristics of Millennials are that they are educated consumers and enjoy working in groups and learning new things on their own. Nearly all of them have played computer games such as Nintendo, X Box, or Playstation at one time or another in their lives.

To this generation, technology is not something new or separate, it is like air. It surrounds them, and they are used to that fact. Many of them have learned to live with it and leverage it for both good and ill. Early members of this generation — the ones we have seen so far in law school — are fairly tolerant of their elders who do not understand and use technology as they do, but it is deeply ingrained in their lives and thinking. While they are generally regarded as being respectful of authority, later members of the generation will likely be less tolerant, and will be more demanding of their teachers.[4]

Members of this generation have caused some consternation to employers.[5] Often, they do not like to be told what to

---

[4] Carlson, THE NET GENERATION GOES TO COLLEGE, CHRON. HIGHER EDUC. (Wash., D.C.), Oct. 7, 2005, at A34; Thomas H. Benton, OH STUPIDITY, PART 2: EXACTLY HOW SHOULD WE TEACH THE DIGITAL NATIVES?, CHRON. HIGHER EDUC. (Wash., D.C.), Sept. 5, 2008, at C1; Diana Oblinger, BOOMERS, GEN-XERS AND MILLENNIALS, UNDERSTANDING THE NEW STUDENTS, EDUCAUSE, July–Aug. 2003, at 37, 38–39.

[5] Darren Garnick, *Surviving Millenial Office Invasion?*, BOSTON HERALD, June 18, 2008, at 24; Morley Safer, *The "Millennials are Coming"* (CBS television broadcast Nov. 11, 2007), *available at* http://www.cbsnews.com/stories/2007/11/08/60minutes/main3475200.shtml; MILLENNIALS THE WORKPLACE: R U READY?, (Mar. 26, 2008), *available at* 2008 WLNR 15510729).

do and want the freedom to be creative. They are also demanding of time off and have a strong desire to balance work with leisure activities. They perceive the zealous dedication to work that their parents exhibited to be unhealthy, often because they saw the results affect their own families — many members of the Millennial Generation have divorced parents.[6]

The Practice of Law

Because the law is based on precedent, the legal profession is by nature conservative and backward looking. Work in law firms used to be slow and ponderous, and often the answer to a business client who wants to try something new or innovative has been a long, expensive memo listing all the risks.

For many years after the advent of personal computers, most attorneys refused to have them in their offices since using them would be considered "secretarial work." Today, the legal profession is increasingly driven by technology and efficiency. As more and more corporate clients have been required to adapt to a globally competitive world, they have demanded similar efficiencies from their attorneys. While 20 years ago many law firms were still resisting significant investments in technology, now no firm can get by without systems of computers. The numbers of laptops and PDAs have increased dramatically in law firms, particularly in the last few years.[7] Clients are demanding immediate access to their attorneys and more and more legal work is conducted via e-mail. The days of the long opinion letter on expensive letterhead stationery are fast fading into the past.

---

[6] Nicolaus Mills, *Don't Ignore Millennials' Virtues*, NEWSDAY, Aug. 12, 2008, at A33. *See also* NEW STRATEGIST PUBL'NS, INC., THE MILLENNIALS: AMERICANS BORN 1977 TO 1994, at 8, tbl. 1.2 (2d ed. 2004).

[7] *See* LEGAL TECH. RES. CTR., AM. BAR ASS'N, 2008 AMERICAN BAR ASSOCIATION LEGAL TECHNOLOGY RESOURCE CENTER SURVEY REPORT: MOBILE LAWYERS TREND REPORT (2008) (hereinafter MOBILE REPORT 2008); LEGAL TECH. RES. CTR., AM. BAR ASS'N, 2006 AMERICAN BAR ASSOCIATION LEGAL TECHNOLOGY RESOURCE CENTER SURVEY REPORT: MOBILE LAWYERS TREND REPORT (2006) [hereinafter MOBILE REPORT 2006].

Increasingly, attorneys need not only to use laptops and PDAs to be more efficient and connected to their clients, but they also need to actually understand how they work. For example, a litigator today can find herself in hot water if she does not handle requests for electronic documents correctly. Just 25 years ago nearly all documents produced in the discovery phase of litigation were on paper. Today, the vast majority of the "documents" we create never take paper form. Because they only live in electronic from litigators must understand how electronic documents are created and stored to properly represent their clients.

With the advent of high-speed global networks, service work of all kinds has moved off-shore and legal work is no exception. Many corporations send routine legal work to large shops of relatively low-paid attorneys in India. Law firms are doing it too — in a recent study, 80 percent of the largest firms admitted to having outsourced projects.[8]

As recently as 30 years ago, many lawyers joined a firm and stayed there for life, but today, loyalty to the firm of one's first employment is nearly gone. This is in part because of increased competition among law firms. Some commentators[9] ascribe this shift in the profession to the publication, starting in 1979, of *The American Lawyer* magazine, which publishes surveys and lists of the top 100 grossing law firms. Prior to the publication of such lists, it was generally not known in the profession what others were making. But with the publication of the survey results, competition to move up the list started in earnest. In the recent past, having a legal career was considered a respectable way to make a modest living. Now partners in the large firms are making seven figure salaries.

But such salaries are increasingly made on the backs of the junior attorneys, who are forced to bill exorbitant

---

[8] William E. Walters, CBA PRESIDENT'S MESSAGE TO MEMBERS: FUTURE LAW — QUO VADIS?, 37 COLO. LAW. 9, 10 (2008).

[9] *See generally* Bruce E. Aronson, ELITE LAW FIRM MERGERS AND REPUTATIONAL COMPETITION: IS BIGGER REALLY BETTER? AN INTERNATIONAL COMPARISON, 40 VAND. J. TRANSNAT'L L. 763, 770–73 (2007); James Regan, HOW ABOUT A FIRM WHERE PEOPLE ACTUALLY WANT TO WORK? A PROFESSIONAL LAW FIRM FOR THE TWENTY-FIRST CENTURY, 69 FORDHAM L. REV. 2693-04 (2001).

numbers of hours per year just to keep their jobs. When you are new to a profession and already under pressure to perform, and also have to bill in excess of 60 hours per week (which means you are typically working 70 or more hours), the pressure is intense. Because the compensation is so high, it is hard to feel sorry for these new associates, but it seems likely that there will be a breaking point in the recent hyper growth of the legal profession.

Given these trends, it is probably not surprising that rates of depression and suicide in the legal profession have increased over the last 30 years.[10] In a study conducted by Johns Hopkins in 1990, lawyers were found to have the highest incidence of depression among the 28 professions covered. A more recent study showed that 19 percent of lawyers surveyed had symptoms of depression and 18 percent abused alcohol.[11] A study conducted by the North Carolina Bar showed 12 percent of depressed lawyers contemplate suicide at least once a month.[12]

Reports on Legal Education, 1914 – 2007

- Redlich Report, 1914
- Reed Report, 1921
- Cramton Report, 1979
- MacCrate Report, 1992
- Carnegie Report, 2007
- CLEA Report, 2007

The Criticism of Legal Education

The form of legal education that exists in most law schools around the country is, simply put, more academic

---

[10] W.W. Eaton et al., OCCUPATIONS AND THE PREVALENCE OF MAJOR DEPRESSIVE DISORDER, 32 J. OCCUPATIONAL MED. 1079–87 (1990).

[11] G. Andrew H. Benjamin et al., THE PREVALENCE OF DEPRESSION, ALCOHOL ABUSE, AND COCAINE ABUSE AMONG UNITED STATE LAWYERS, 13 INT'L J. L. & PSYCHIATRY 233–46 (1990).

[12] Michael J. Sweeney, Am. Bar Ass'n, THE DEVASTATION OF DEPRESSION: LAWYERS AT GREATER RISK, BAR LEADER, Mar.–Apr. 1998, at 11.

than practical. This has been the subject of criticism for nearly 100 years. The Carnegie Foundation for the Advancement of Teaching, an institution that has long enjoyed broad respect in higher education, issued a report in 1914 that recommended a more holistic and contextualized approach be taken in educating lawyers and preparing them for the practice of law. Just four years before that, the Carnegie Foundation issued what became known as the Flexner Report, which made a similar recommendation for medical education. The current system of clinical supervision and internships building to a medical residency was born out of that report. Medical education changed based on the Carnegie Foundation's recommendations, but for the most part legal education did not.

Indeed, even as recently as 20 years ago, it was generally accepted that newly-minted law school graduates were so lacking in practical expertise that the firms they joined had to train them in the specifics of the law and in local rules, and the firms generally accepted this responsibility. But now, largely because of the increasingly competitive environment of the legal profession, firms are less and less interested in taking on this role. Also, with annual salaries for new attorneys ballooning in some cities to $150,000 and more, firms tend understandably to be less patient with new associates who need significant training before they are truly useful.

In 1992, the American Bar Association's Task Force on Legal Education and the Profession produced a report that is informally named for the chair of that panel, the "MacCrate Report." It recommended that legal education focus its efforts on the teaching of ten "skills and values" it deemed essential to the practice of law. While the MacCrate Report generated some discussion, legal education remained substantially the same.

More recently, however, there has been considerable movement on this front. The Carnegie Foundation issued another report in 2007 that, although supportive of some aspects of legal education, was critical of others. In the same year, the Clinical Legal Education Association issued a similarly negative assessment. Most of the criticisms in these reports were no surprise to anyone in the legal academy, but the respect paid to the Carnegie Foundation and CLEA, and the quality of their reports, joined with considerable inchoate concerns among many law school faculty members to cause a more serious engagement with the criticisms than ever before. In the year following the publication of these later reports, there were a number of conferences where legal educators discussed them, and there were numerous announcements of curricular changes from schools trying to respond.

Also influential has been the Law School Survey of Student Engagement (LSSSE), which is conducted annually by the Indiana University Center for Postsecondary Research. This organization has issued a series of annual reports describing the results of its survey of law students at 148 different law schools. One of the most striking points made each year by the LSSSE is the large number of third year students who disengage from their studies. In the 2007 report, 21 percent of 3L students said they "frequently" came to class unprepared. They were also less than satisfied with the law school experience overall.[13]

The Curricular Experiments

In response to all this criticism a number of schools have implemented or announced various significant curricular changes. Washington & Lee School of Law eliminated its third year of classes, replacing it with an entirely clinical year. Harvard Law School changed its 1L curriculum significantly to pay more attention to the rise of the administrative state in legal practice. Indiana University Law School announced that all 1L students would be taking a new course in "the economics and values of the profession."

What is interesting about these changes — and there are many others being tried — is they are all happening at once. For the first time in more than 100 years, there seems to be a widespread and growing recognition that there is a serious problem in legal education that needs to be addressed, and for the first time ever there is urgency to it.

---

[13] Ctr. for Postsecondary Research, Annual Law School Survey of Student Engagement 19 (2007).

Unfortunately, while many of these curricular reforms seem like good ideas, they also seem rather haphazard. They are reminiscent of what one of the authors of the Carnegie report, William M. Sullivan, wrote: "... efforts to improve legal education have been more piecemeal than comprehensive."[14] Sullivan was referring to the past, but this particular criticism seems to still be true. At least so far, reforms have been partial and haphazard. And it is not clear that these curricular changes involve any attempt to teach the new subjects in different ways. Indeed, Sullivan's doubts have recently been echoed by Dean Erwin Chemerinsky of UC Irvine Law School when he wrote: "... adding new courses taught in traditional ways does not significantly alter legal education."[15]

Further, many of the more significant curricular changes are reaching small groups of students and show no evidence of being scalable to larger numbers. Worse, none of these curricular changes leverage technology in any coordinated fashion as part of the curricular design. And none of them seem to recognize that law schools are dealing with a new kind of student, the Millennials for whom technology is central to their lives, and for whom technology will be vital to their lives as practicing attorneys.

But the depth of the discussion itself is significant, and it will play a role in the coming of the "Perfect Storm."

The Humanizing Movement

Another sort of criticism has also been focused recently on legal education, namely that it has not only been failing to properly prepare students for practice, but also has actually been dehumanizing them. Critics concerned with this problem have gathered under the banner of Humanizing Legal Education and in 2007 and 2008 they held meetings to discuss it. These critics believe that by its very design legal

---

[14] WILLIAM M. SULLIVAN ET AL., CARNEGIE FOUND. FOR THE ADVANCEMENT OF TEACHING, EDUCATING LAWYERS: PREPARATION FOR THE PROFESSION OF LAW, 189–90 (2007) [hereinafter CARNEGIE 2007].

[15] Erwin Chemerinksky, RETHINKING LEGAL EDUCATION, 43 HARV. C.R.-C.L. L. REV. 595, 595 (2008).

education separates students from their core values and thereby contributes to unhappy lawyers and, ultimately, to a dysfunctional profession.

One element of these discussions centers around the psychological concept of "autonomy." Some compelling research shows that students who attended a law school that was supportive of its student's autonomy — that is, treated them as mature human beings with their own feelings and ideas — performed far better on the bar examination than those who attended a school that was less supportive. This result is striking because the students who passed the bar examination at higher rates had gone to a lower ranked school.

Much more research needs to be done in this area. What is important is that this type of research is being conducted, and there is a growing group of legal educators who are deeply concerned about the form and process of legal education, not just its content. And they are making some compelling arguments about the need for significant change. This too will play a role in the coming Perfect Storm.

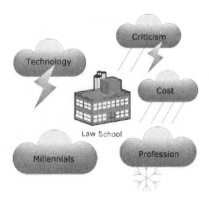

The March of Technology

Perhaps most compelling is the role that technology is playing in the lives of the law students of today and will play in the future. It permeates their lives, and has increasingly been employed in their high school and college courses in innovative and effective ways. They will increasingly come to expect the same in their legal education.

It is highly probable that the legal careers enjoyed by today's students will change direction because of yet more sophisticated technologies developed during the course of their careers, and likely more than once. The current forms of teaching in law school are not sufficient to prepare students for the technological challenges they will face in the 21st Century. Fortunately, developing technology — particularly Web 2.0 technology — is creating and supporting a new form of participation and communication that are ideal for many of the sorts of changes being discussed in legal education.

A simple way of describing this development is found in some terminology being used in education circles: the difference between "learning about" and "learning to be." The former, which historically has been widely accepted in much of education, posits that knowledge is a substance and teaching is about transfer of that substance. But the emerging social view of learning posits that understanding is — especially for the new generation — socially constructed.[16] While basic knowledge is certainly important — without it we have no discipline of law — what will be equally important in the careers for which we are preparing our students is the socially constructed understanding of what it means to be a lawyer.

Put another way, the students of the future will need to know not just how to "think like a lawyer" — the traditional pedagogical goal — but how to "act like and be a lawyer." To effectively do this, we will have to invent "Legal Pedagogy 2.0" where, at a minimum, we teachers become less "the sage on the stage" and more "the guide on the side." Merely transferring content from the podium to expectant student containers is insufficient. The old approach is based on the out of date assumption that information is scarce when that is no longer true. It will not connect with the new generation of law students, and it will insufficiently employ the benefits of technology for teaching and communicating effectively with them. Worse, and it will insufficiently prepare them for the practice in which they are going to live and grow. The changes being discussed are profound and cannot be accomplished

---

[16] *See generally* John Seely Brown & Richard P. Adler, *Minds on Fire*, EDUCAUSE REV., Jan.–Feb. 2008, at 17–32.

without leveraging emerging technologies. Fortunately, the need and the means are coming together at the same time.

Conclusion

There is an analogy often used in business circles about the many companies that, a 100 and more years ago made horse-drawn carriages. When Henry Ford's Model T car started to be mass produced, the carriage companies failed to recognize and react to the threat, and consequently went out of business. This analogy has been applied to the recording industry; the growth of the digital distribution of music has had costly, profound and far-reaching effects. When the American recording industry chose to fight rather than innovate, it ended up protecting a shrinking asset while Apple built iTunes.

It is tempting to make a similar analogy here — that legal education, if it does not innovate, will find itself with the horse and buggy companies. Protective mechanisms, especially ABA accreditation and control, will (as long as they survive) limit this threat.

There is, though, a better analogy. The change from the horse carriage to the Model T automobile was a significant technological progression, but both technologies were about getting us to the same place. The automobile just got us there faster and more efficiently than the horse. Today, for all its innovation, iTunes distributes music, just in a different form and through a different mechanism than before.

The better analogy for legal education in the 21st Century is the automobile compared to a rocket ship. We can continue to refine the automobile. But automotive technology 100 years later is still about the same thing: internal combustion engines getting us from one place to another — and one that is much the same as the place we left (in many cases, with a strip mall nearby and a Starbucks on every corner).

The space shuttle was built to get us to an entirely new place that looks and operates very differently from where we are today. The change that is needed in legal education is not just another form of the same place we have already been, with a few tweaks here and there. It is more along the lines of the space shuttle — we need to harness more complex technology than we are currently familiar with to get legal education to the very different place it needs to be before the end of this century. Fortunately, many elements are coming together all at once that will help make that happen. Web technology and its influence on teaching and students, combined with changes in the legal profession and the timing of broad and detailed criticisms of legal education, creates a situation that is ripe for significant change. Today, the chance that legal education can again resist the combination and timing of these forces seems remote.

Further Reading

GENE KOO, NEW SKILLS, NEW LEARNING: LEGAL EDUCATION & THE PROMISE OF TECHNOLOGY (2007).

U.S. DEP'T OF EDUC., TOWARD A NEW GOLDEN AGE IN EDUCATION: HOW THE INTERNET, THE LAW AND TODAY'S STUDENTS ARE REVOLUTIONIZING EXPECTATIONS, NATIONAL EDUCATION TECHNOLOGY PLAN (2004).

EDUCATING THE NET GEN (Diana G. Olinger et al. eds., 2005).

Chapter 3

THE MILLENNIAL GENERATION

In a book that is largely about the power of technology to transform legal education, it would probably be a good thing to define what technology is. This is difficult to do because the word describes a target that is constantly moving. Perhaps the best definition was provided more than 20 years ago by the famous technologist Alan Kay who worked at the Xerox PARC lab out of which came the first graphical user interface and mouse. "Technology," Kay said, "is anything that was invented after you were born."[17] For our purposes, this is as good a definition as any. Of course, to our great

---

[17] Quoted in EDUCATION AND TECHNOLOGY: CRITICAL PERSPECTIVES, POSSIBLE FUTURES 194 (David W. Witt & Lucien T. Winegar eds., 2007).

grandfathers the automobile was technology. So were the radio and the zipper. But to those of us living today neither the car nor the radio seem like technology at all. They were never novel to us; they have always been there. But to most members of the "Baby Boom" generation, computers and cell phones are technology.

By contrast, members of the Millennial Generation, born in 1982 or later, have always lived in a world where the personal computer existed; indeed, 1982 began with the mass production of the first IBM PC (which made its debut in August of 1981). The precursor to the laptop of today, the Compaq Portable (which was about the size of a large suitcase and not very portable at all) was unveiled in November of 1982, and soon thereafter IBM-compatible machines from various manufacturers became increasingly available. As a result, during the entirety of the lives of our students it has been possible to use a word processor to create a document and to calculate numbers on a computerized spreadsheet. Likewise it has always been possible to play a computer game. Members of this generation have no memory of a time when these things were not possible because they always have been.

The Internet, although available earlier to academic institutions, became available to the general public in the early to mid-1990s, when the youngest members of the Millennial Generation were 12 years old. Members of that generation who entered law school in 2008 were even younger — they were only 8 years old in the mid-1990s. Effectively, for nearly all the members of this generation that are currently in or about to enter law school, the Internet has been part of the landscape. It is no more "technology" to them than the automobile is to us. To them it is like the air they breathe.

A recent study by the U.S. Department of Education found that, as of 2005, 90 percent of students between the ages of 5 and 17 used computers, and that most teenagers spent more time online than watching television. Further, 94 percent of online teenagers used the Internet for school-related research. Perhaps the most astonishing statistic is this one: between 2000 and 2002 the largest group of users to log onto the Internet for the first time were between the ages of two and five.[18]

The availability of the Internet in the classroom is a more recent phenomenon. In 1996, second grade students had classroom Internet connectivity at a rate of only 14 percent. That number jumped to 51 percent in 1998, and by 2002, it had increased to 92 percent.[19]

One thing these numbers indicate is that although members of the Millennial Generation are used to technology, having computers as a part of the classroom experience is relatively new. This means two things. One is that those of

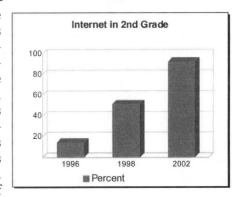

us who teach in law schools have some time to get up to speed on the classroom use of computers. A student who was in second grade in 2002 will not enter law school until 2017 (at the earliest). It also means that in only five-plus years we will have students who will think it very strange to be told that they cannot use their laptops in class.

The Department of Education study examined the pervasiveness of technology in education and the new level of enthusiasm that it is generating. The report noted this:

> "We have clearly reached a turning point. All over this country, we see evidence of a new excitement in education, a new determination, a hunger for change. The technology that has so dramatically changed the world outside our schools is now

[18] U.S. Dep't of Educ., Toward a New Golden Age in Education: How the Internet, the Law and Today's Students are Revolutionizing Expectations, National Education Technology Plan, nn. 28–34 (2004) [hereinafter Technology Plan].

[19] Mark R. Nelson, E Books in Higher Education, Educause Review, Mar.–Apr. 2008, at 50.

changing the learning and teaching environment within them. Sometimes this is driven by the students themselves, born and comfortable in the age of the Internet. There has been explosive growth in the availability of online instruction and virtual schools, complementing traditional instruction with high quality courses tailored to the needs of individual students."[20]

Various studies of and reports about the Millennial Generation indicate that, in addition to computers and the Internet being an integral part of their lives, they possess several characteristics that are important for legal educators to know. First, they are generally respectful of authority. (For those of us who remember struggling to teach members of the previous generation, known as Generation X, this seems comforting). Second, the Millennials are more accepting of other cultures and races than previous generations. Third, they believe it is "cool to be smart." Fourth, they like the benefits of working in community, and find online communities, text messaging, and Instant Messaging (IM) to be particularly convenient and efficient methods of communication.[21] Lastly, many members of this generation have been protected and celebrated by their parents, and are used to having them closely involved in their lives even through college. This has led to a pejorative term "helicopter parents," a reference to how they drop in anywhere and any time to watch over their children in school.

It should be noted that, although members of this generation are, as some refer to them, "digital natives," that does not mean they are always digitally literate. Digital natives were born into the connected world and it is second nature to them, but that does not mean they use the tools well, appropriately or optimally. Some need to be reminded that putting embarrassing photos on Facebook is not wise. Others need to understand better how their e-mail

---

[20] TECHNOLOGY PLAN, *supra* note 18, at 35.

[21] Alicia Moore, *They've Never Taken a Swim and Thought About Jaws: Understanding the Millenial Generation*, College & University 82:4 2007, p. 41, available at: http://www.pacrao.org/docs/resources/writersteam/UnderstandingTheMillennialGeneration.doc.

communications come across to the reader, particularly in a professional setting. And they all need to understand how to use the tools they know to enhance and enable learning what they do not know. There is still much that we can teach them.

The Hypertext Mind

While all of the characteristics of Millennials listed above have important implications for legal educators, perhaps the most important is this generation's comfort with learning in non-traditional learning environments. As previously noted, a significant shift in teaching and learning is already taking place in high schools and colleges. This shift is often described as a transition from a "teacher-centered" approach to a "learning-centered" one.

In a teacher-centered approach, the teacher's mission is thought to be simply about transferring knowledge. Learning is viewed as linear and cumulative. In contrast, a learning-centered approach is one where students are involved in the discovery and construction of knowledge, and where learning is perceived as non-linear.[22] Parker Palmer, in his well-known book *The Courage to Teach*, refers to the teacher-centered approach as the "objectivist" model of learning. He describes the limitations of such an approach, and en-courages teachers to shift to a "community of truth" model, where the subject (not the teacher) is the center of the community, and all participants in the class — including the teacher — are learning from each other.

The important connection to be made between this shift in teaching models and the growth of the Internet is that they follow one another very closely, and they fit together. The Web, of course, is constructed on the concept of hypertext, with infinite and non-linear connections between related types of knowledge. Hypertext is by definition non-linear; indeed, it is designed to support discovery and construction

---

[22] Robert Barr & John Tagg, FROM TEACHING TO LEARNING — A NEW PARADIGM FOR UNDERGRADUATE EDUCATION, CHANGE, ETC., 27 CHANGE 12–25 (Nov./Dec. 1995); David A Whetten, PRINCIPLES OF EFFECTIVE COURSE DESIGN: WHAT I WISH I HAD KNOWN ABOUT LEARNING-CENTERED TEACHING 30 YEARS AGO, 31 J. MGMT. EDUC. 339 (2007).

of knowledge by the user through the interlinking of related documents.

It could thus be argued that increasingly students entering law school will not only have had greater experience with a learning-centered approach in their prior schooling, but also with minds that have been formed, at least in part, by the experience of learning in a hypertextual way. When students with this sort of "hypertext mind" enter law school and find themselves thrust into an environment that is primarily linear, the clash will be significant. To students with hypertext-formed minds, the idea of a printed book which we are asking them to read from page 1 to page 500 (in that order) will be increasingly foreign.

Rand J. Shapiro, a professor of educational psychology at Michigan State University who has made a study of Internet-based reading by teenagers, was recently quoted in an article in the New York Times about the decline in book reading among teenagers: "[Young people] aren't as troubled as some of us older folks are by reading that doesn't go in a line. That's a good thing because the world doesn't go in a line and isn't organized into separate compartments or chapters."[23] That sounds true, and increasingly so, of the legal and business world our graduates are going into.

One could argue that there is something special about the law that requires a linear progression. And there are no doubt some examples of this. It can be said that a particular section of Article 2 of the UCC needs to be understood first before one can properly understand the next (and subsequent) sections. That may be true, but there are several questions raised by this view. First, is that relationship simply an artifact of the linear mind that drafted Article 2? Second, will all laws continue to be drafted in this way? Is some particular clarity offered by such a format? More importantly, do we really read statutes in this way? Usually, what leads us in practice to a statute is a client problem, and we often find ourselves studying the middle of the statute before we have had a chance to back out and look at the forest rather than the trees. Why not teach statutes in this way, emphasizing

---

[23] Motoko Rich, LITERACY DEBATE: ONLINE, RU REALLY READING?, N.Y. TIMES, July 27, 2008, at A1.

connections across and between the linear progressions of the statute's drafter?

Indeed, much of the law is in fact hypertextual. The case reporter system, and particularly Lexis' star pagination and West's keynote system, can be said to be the precursor to the hypertext environment we now call the Web. It is not a stretch to suggest, therefore, that students with greater facility and comfort with the hypertextual nature of everything they learn will take to this aspect of the law with greater facility than earlier students have. Perhaps the arrival of the hypertext mind in law schools will be a good thing for us, for our teaching, and for the legal practice our students will enter.

The Participatory Culture

Another salient aspect of the Millennials is their comfort with — even assumption of — collaborative work and online communities. Much of this comfort has come from the ubiquity of technologies that support this sort of co-creation and community such as Facebook and MySpace. In 2007 the Pew Internet and American Life project[24] reported that more than half of all American teens had created a blog or webpage and had posted original artwork, photography or videos online. Most had done more than one of these activities. It also reported that 22 percent of teens have their own websites and 19 percent blog.[25]

A 2006 report from the MacArthur Foundation applied the term "participatory culture" to describe the world the Millennials will live in.[26] According to the report, elements of the participatory culture include, affiliations (joining various online communities), expressions (creating content in various forms), collaborative problem-solving (working together in teams, both formal and informal), and circulations

---

[24] THE PEW RESEARCH CTR., HOW YOUNG PEOPLE VIEW THEIR LIVES, FUTURES AND POLITICS: A PORTRAIT OF "GENERATION NEXT" (2007).

[25] HENRY JENKINS ET AL., MACARTHUR FOUND., CONFRONTING THE CHALLENGES OF PARTICIPATORY CULTURE: MEDIA EDUCATION FOR THE 21ST CENTURY 6 (2006), *available at* http://www.macfound.org/site/apps/nlnet/content3.aspx?c=lkLXJ8MQKrH&b=4201377&ct=2946895.

[26] *Id.*

(shaping the flow of media, such as through a blog). While the typical law school experience addresses some of these elements, such as collaborative problem-solving (and legal writing is, of course, a form of expression), the experience currently remains limited in most of them.

The MacArthur report delineates eleven cultural competencies and social skills that will be needed for full involvement in the participatory culture: play (experimenting with one's surroundings), performance (adopting alternative identities for the purpose of discovery), simulation (interpreting dynamic models of real-world processes), appropriation (sampling and re-mixing media content), multitasking (shifting focus as needed on salient details), distributed cognition (interacting with tools that expand mental capacities), collective intelligence (pooling knowledge and comparing notes with others), judgment (evaluating reliability and credibility of different information sources), transmedia navigation (following the flow of information across multiple modalities), networking (searching for and synthesizing information), and negotiation (discerning and respecting multiple perspectives).

MacArthur Foundation – Cultural Competencies

- Play
- Performance
- Simulation
- Appropriation
- Distributed Cognition
- Multitasking
- Collective Intelligence
- Judgment
- Transmedia Navigation
- Networking
- Negotiation

Of these eleven cultural competencies, the typical law school experience attends to as few as three of them or as many as five if the student participates in a clinic. The law school classroom does not typically enable play, simulation, appropriation, collective intelligence, or transmedia navigation, and it actively discourages multitasking. We do better at distributed cognition, judgment, and networking, and if a student has a clinical or practicum experience, he or she will be exposed to Performance and Negotiation. Students, generally on their own initiative, construct collective intelligence in study groups and other co-curricular activities.

Supporting only three out of eleven cultural competencies our students will need is simply inadequate. Even five out of eleven is not very good. If one accepts that the world our students live in today is increasingly a participatory culture, and further that the world they will be practicing law in will also be participatory in nature, then we should address some of these deficiencies. Fortunately, because so many of these elements and characteristics are enabled by technology, the same technologies can help us bring these elements into the law school classroom.

In his book *Here Comes Everybody*, Clay Shirky explains how the participatory culture has changed, and will continue to change, the action of groups in our society:

> For most of modern life, our strong talents and desires for group effort have been filtered through relatively rigid institutional structures because of the complexity of managing groups. We haven't had all the groups we wanted, we've simply had all the groups we could afford. The old limits of what unmanaged and unpaid groups can do are no longer in operation: the difficulties that kept self-assembled groups from working together are shrinking, meaning that the number and kinds of things groups can get done without financial motivation or managerial oversight are growing. The current change, in one sentence, is this: most of the barriers to group action have collapsed, and without those barriers, we are free to explore new ways of gathering together and getting things done.[27]

---

[27] CLAY SHIRKY, HERE COMES EVERYBODY, THE POWER OF ORGANIZING WITHOUT ORGANIZATIONS 21–22 (2008).

Members of the Millennial Generation know this instinc-
tively since many of them have already experienced, or
experimented with, these sorts of groups. The implications of
this shift are profound for legal education. We not only must
prepare our students for this different world, we must be
aware of the nature of the threat that it represents to our
institutions. Indeed, anyone who makes their living as a part
of an institution that creates groups (such as a law school)
might feel threatened by this development. But as Shirky goes
on to explain, we still need institutions. We just have to deal
with more competition: "Though some of the early utopian-
ism around new communications tools suggested that we
were heading into some sort of post-hierarchical paradise,
that's not what's happening now, and it's not what's going to
happen. None of the absolute advantages of institutions like
businesses or schools or governments have disappeared.
Instead, what has happened is that most of the *relative*
advantages of those institutions have disappeared — relative,
that is, to the direct effort of the people they represent."[28]

The potential affect of this shift on society as a whole is
profound. Every place groups get together will be affected by
this change, and this includes law schools. It will be far better
to learn about this change and consider its effect on our
institutions, than to wake up surprised after it is too late.

These themes are also emphasized in *Wikinomics: How
Mass Collaboration Changes Everything* by Dan Tapscott
and Anthony Williams. In their book — which primarily
focuses on how collaboration and the Internet have changed
the business world — the authors explain that the Web is now
a "ubiquitous platform for computation and collaboration
that is reshaping nearly every aspect of human affairs. ...
Twenty years from now we will look back at this period of the
early twenty-first century as a critical turning point in
economic and social history."[29] Since many of our graduates
will work for businesses either directly or through a law firm,
this change must have an effect on what we are doing in legal
education.

---

[28] *Id.* at 23.

[29] Don Tapscott & Anthony D. Williams, Wikinomics: How Mass
Collaboration Changes Everything, 19 (2006).

In his book *The Wisdom of Crowds* James Surowiecki advances the theory that the sort of collaboration supported by Web 2.0 technologies often creates better results than any individual or group of individuals could create on their own. Since communal sites are likely to be a fixture of the world we are preparing our students to join, why would we not look for applications of such technology to aid in their preparation?

All of this has already reached a massive scale, and continues to grow every day. There are now more than one billion CPUs on the Internet and eight terabytes of traffic per *second*, including two million e-mails. There are three billion cell phone users in the world.[30] Recently, China surpassed the United States in the number of Internet users with 253 million. Astonishingly, that represents only 19 percent of China's population while 70 percent of the population of the United States is already online.[31] The generation that will be entering law school over the next decade knows how big this is getting and places great faith in community action and online networking to support its growth. They are steeped in the connected, participatory culture. We simply must learn to embrace this reality and harness it for improvement in what we offer our students. Eventually, they will demand it.

The Millennials in Politics

There is mounting evidence that the Millennials are beginning to make their presence known in politics, as E. J. Dionne, a columnist for the *Washington Post* noted in an opinion piece. He cited a report from the Center for Information Research on Civil Learning and Engagement: "Electoral participation among 18–24 year olds increased from 36 percent in 2000 to 47 percent in 2004."[32] More recently, he noted, in the 2008 primaries 17 percent of those under 30 turned out, as compared to 9 percent in 2000. While some of this increase may have been caused by the

---

[30] Louis Rossetto, *Letter to Orson and Zoe*, WIRED, May 2008, at 175.

[31] David Barboza, *China Surpasses U.S. in Number of Internet Users,* N.Y. TIMES, July 26, 2008, at B3.

[32] E.J. Dionne, Jr., *The Year the Youth Vote Arrives*, WASH. POST, July 25, 2008, at A21.

excitement surrounding the candidacy of Barack Obama at least one commentator has called the increase in political interest among the young "staggering."[33]

Dionne concludes his article by praising the potential of this generation to make a difference in politics: "Young Americans show all the signs of being interested enough and upset enough to flock to the polls this year. If they do, they could be the most politically consequential generation since the cohort of the Great Depression and World War II. Think of these newcomers as the Engaged Generation."[34]

In his book *Youth to Power, How Today's Young Voters Are Building Tomorrow's Progressive Majority*, Michael Connery[35] makes a similar argument. He credits this generation's comfort with forming online communities, and the Internet's efficient ways of supporting such communities, as enabling and energizing significant civic involvement.

But perhaps the best thing is to let members of the generation speak for themselves on this topic. There are several political blogs authored and run by Millennials. Two of the more prominent ones send a message simply through the names they have adopted: Futuremajority and Pushback. One announcement began like this:

> A lot has been made of Millennial participation in this year's political primary season, but little of it has actually been written by the Millennials. That's about to change at a new blog called Pushback: Young people today are becoming politically engaged at a faster rate than any other demographic. We are developing many of the online tools politicians use to spread their messages. We are starting non-profits and NGOs. We are organizing campaigns or running for office ourselves. As we look around the world we are about to inherit, our concerns are becoming more urgent — and harder to ignore. Yet the media

---

[33] *Id.*

[34] *Id.*

[35] MICHAEL CONNERY, YOUTH TO POWER, HOW TODAY'S YOUNG VOTERS ARE BUILDING TOMORROW'S PROGRESSIVE MAJORITY (2008).

and right-wing politicians insist on treating us like some sort of bizarre alien tribe. They decry youth culture, present jaded views of what young people stand for, and, worst of all, speak for us instead of letting us speak for ourselves. That's why we've started Pushback, a blog written and edited by a diverse group of progressive young people from across the country. Pushback's goal is simple: Let young people speak for themselves, not just on stereotypically "youth-oriented" topics like music and celebrities, but on everything from healthcare to congressional races to American foreign policy. We can't stop those who continue to stereotype and attack us. But we can push back, and that's why we're here.[36]

The Criticism of the Millennials

Given the nature of these changes and the pressures they present, it is not surprising that some members of an older generation have taken it upon themselves to criticize many characteristics of the Millennials. It is a trope as ancient as time itself, with the older members of society finding fault with the more youthful ones. Today's seniors are no exception. They have excoriated the Millennials for being narcissistic, watching too much TV or spending too much time playing video games. Or that they do not read enough or write enough, and are bad at both.

Adding to the chorus of complaints is a recent book provocatively entitled *The Dumbest Generation* by Mark Bauerlein.[37] In it Bauerlein posits that the digital age has dumbed down the Millennials. He marshals various studies showing that they do not read print books as much as prior generations and that their preference toward multitasking has shortened their attention spans. Bauerlein dredges up

---

[36] *See* Pushback.org, *About Us,* http://www.pushback.org/about/ (last visited Oct. 4, 2008) (explaining mission statement of pushback.org).

[37] MARK BAUERLEIN, THE DUMBEST GENERATION: HOW THE DIGITAL AGE STUPIFIES YOUNG AMERICANS AND JEOPARDIZES OUR FUTURE (OR, DON'T TRUST ANYONE UNDER 30) (2008).

examples of young folks not knowing enough about geography or unable to identify the Pope. He laments how saturated with the celebrity culture they are. Bauerlein then goes on to criticize much of the growing literature supporting the entry of technology into the classroom as being driven by student preferences rather than hard science. He leaps from these attacks on the young to this concluding broadside:

> Adults everywhere need to align against youth ignorance and apathy. ... The moral poles need to reverse, with the young no longer setting the pace for right conduct and cool thinking. Let's tell the truth. The Dumbest Generation will cease being dumb only when it regards adolescence as an inferior realm of petty strivings and adulthood as a realm of civic, historical, and cultural awareness that puts them in touch with the perennial ideas and struggles. The youth of America occupy a point in history like every other generation did and will, and their time will end. But the effects of their habits will outlast them, and if things do not change they will be remembered as the fortunate ones who were unworthy of the privileges they inherited. They may even be recalled as the generation that lost that great American heritage, forever.[38]

Putting aside how revealing this broadside is of Bauerlein's own agenda, it should be noted that many of his observations are true of the culture at large. Most of us are distracted by our cell phones. Many of us spend too much time in front of a TV, and we do not read as much as we should or wish we could. Even some older people become mesmerized by their computer screens and spend countless hours browsing and emailing. Polemical books such as Bauerlein's pander to our fears and they sell very well. They are just too comforting when we find ourselves occasionally frustrated with our students, who every fall have the unfortunate habit of reminding us that we are one year older and that much further removed from their experience.

---

[38] *Id.* at 236.

Further, much of the criticism of the younger generation by Bauerlein and others is at least premature. The earliest Millennials are only in their mid-twenties and most are still in their teens. To accuse them of jeopardizing the nation and of not having saved the world seems a bit silly, at best. Teenagers throughout history have often wasted some of their time being teenagers. That does not prove that they did not eventually grow up.

More to the point here, since this book is about legal education, the students who get into law school are generally the "cream of the crop." They have usually done very well in college, and most of them did well enough in high school before that to be accepted into a competitive college. So for the most part they were wasting their teen years far less than the rest of their peers and it seems safe to say they read a few books in the process of their education. While they may have shorter attention spans than students in the past, and they may not have read as much classical literature as some of us did in college, they are typically not examples of the youth at which much of this criticism is directed.

More important, these criticisms of the Millennials are mostly a waste of time. For our purposes it is better to think of the characteristics of this generation as neither bad nor good — they just are. Trying to alter their behavior is reminiscent of that lesson in love most of us have had to learn at some point in our lives: do not get into a relationship with someone unsuitable in the hope that you can change them. This does not mean, of course, that we should give up trying to teach our students — and through that, perhaps, to help them modify their own behaviors. What is important is that, instead of criticizing them, we need to understand them so we can teach them more effectively. Grumbling about TV and the Internet gets us nowhere. Furthermore, if we are to start each year with the mentality that our students are one year dumber than we are, then we are likely to be less effective teachers of them. The fact is, most of us find the new 1L enrollees we meet every fall to be bright, hard working and energetic students. Sure, we wish most of them could write better, and that they understood some things about the world better than they do. But that is why they need us.

Further Reading

NEIL HOWE & WILLIAM STRAUSS, MILLENNIALS RISING: THE NEXT GREAT GENERATION (2000).

DON TAPSCOTT & ANTHONY D. WILLIAMS, WIKINOMICS: HOW MASS COLLABORATION CHANGES EVERYTHING (2006).

CLAY SHIRKY, HERE COMES EVERYBODY: THE POWER OF ORGANIZING WITHOUT ORGANIZATIONS (2008).

PARKER PALMER, THE COURAGE TO TEACH: EXPLORING THE INNER LANDSCAPE OF A TEACHER'S LIFE (2007)

Chapter 4

THE PRACTICE OF LAW

In some ways the practice of law is the same as it has ever been. Generally clients do not hire lawyers to handle the easy problems. Instead they bring the hard problems to lawyers, the tough things that take time and expertise to sort out. They pay us to handle the intricate problems of complex real estate transactions, of product liability defense, of figuring out who the responsible parties at a Superfund site are and how to get them to pay to clean it up. Because of this, lawyering will always be a difficult and stressful job. A certain amount of stress has always gone with the territory. Beyond this common baseline, however, the practice of law is dramatically different than it was when legal education started more than 100 years ago.

While lawyers still do a lot of the same things they have always done, the last 40 years have brought significant change to the practice of law. As with most things in our society, fundamental skills have remained essential to the legal field today, but they are being stretched and added to more than ever before. There are several reasons for this. First and foremost is the rise of the Administrative state. The explosion of regulation that started in the 1960s has given rise to a greater need for attorneys to sort it all out. Virtually every product offered for sale in the United States (and in the EU and most industrialized countries) has some sort of regulatory implication whether it relates to the actual manufacture of the product, the transportation of it, or the point of its sale, and usually all three.

Simply looking at the growth in the Gross National Product one can see how dramatically bigger business has become and this has naturally affected lawyers. In 1970 the GNP was $1.04 trillion. In 2007 it had grown to $13.9 trillion. This sort of growth, and the regulatory complexity that came with it, has done more than just increase the number of lawyers. It is simply a much more complex regulatory and business world today than it was in 1970. The idea that virtually the same sort of legal education we had in 1970 would still fit the much bigger and more complex world we live in today is at least dubious on its face.

Not surprisingly, there has been a tremendous growth in technology spending by businesses, which now must have sophisticated computer networks to stay competitive. In 2006, spending in the United States on technology was $983 Billion. In 2007 that number increased to $1.009 trillion. Forrester Research has projected that in 2008 global technology spending will reach $1.7 trillion, a 6 percent growth rate over 2007.[39]

There is simply no doubting that the business world is now heavily dependent on computers and other technology, and that technology has enabled its massive growth. The Forrester report predicts that the next wave of technological growth in business will involve moving beyond automating existing business functions and into "using technology, especially analytics software, to optimize business results."

---

[39] Andrew Bartels et al., *Global IT 2008 Market Outlook*, Feb. 11, 2008, *available at*: http://www.forrester.com/Research/Document/Excerpt/0,7211,44429,00.html.

Over the last 40 years as large companies have grown larger they have gathered into conglomerates, and lawyers have been there to navigate the shoals of regulation that applied to the mergers. As the conglomerates have increasingly conducted business outside of the United States, lawyers have had to learn more international law than was necessary in the past.[40]

One of the results of this immense growth in the law is that it has lead to a concomitant growth of specialization. Except in small towns it is virtually impossible now to be a generalist attorney. You are a tax attorney or a real estate attorney or an environmental attorney or an international lawyer. And, typically, once you specialize you remain in that specialty the rest of your career.

With a few notable exceptions, specialist attorneys cannot survive on their own. They need to work for large firms that attract large clients who have complex issues that require several specialists to sort out, especially the regulatory thickets that stand in the way of the corporation's manufacture, transport or sale of its goods. And so an important feature in the last 30 years has been the growth of the mega firm. In 1980 the largest 25 law firms in the United States ranged in size from 187 to 544 attorneys.[41] As of 2007 there were 25 law firms with more than 1,000 attorneys, and most of these firms had at least a dozen offices around the world.[42]

As a perhaps inevitable result of these trends, many attorneys report deep dissatisfaction with the practice of law. In a recent study conducted by the American Bar Association, 44 percent of lawyers said they would not recommend the profession to a young person.[43] The practice of law has also experienced a decline in its prestige over the last two decades

---

[40] Steve Lohr, *Corporate Tech Spending: What's Next*, N.Y. TIMES BITS BLOG, Feb. 12, 2008, *available at*: http://bits.blogs.nytimes.com/2008/02/12/corporate-tech-spending-whats-next/.

[41] National Law Firm Survey, NAT'L L.J., Oct. 6, 1980, at 32–37.

[42] The NLJ250, NAT'L L.J., Nov. 12, 2007, at S18.

[43] Alex Williams, *The Falling-Down Professions*, N.Y. TIMES, Jan. 6, 2008, at section 9, 1.

and as we have noted before, there has been a huge increase in the number of attorneys suffering from depression.[44]

Gaining strength is the view that not only has the practice of law changed in recent years, but also that it is threatened, at least in the form we have known it. In a 2007 issue of *The Stanford Lawyer*, the Dean of Stanford Law School, Larry Kramer, wrote: "I have occasionally remarked, though only in small settings before today, that the state of the legal profession brings to mind Rome, circa A.D. 300. On the surface, it looks grander and more magnificent than ever. But the foundation may be about to collapse. It's meant to be a joke. But the uneasy laugh this comment invariably elicits suggests that it may be closer to the mark than any of us wishes."[45]

The Rise of Technology in the Practice

Not surprisingly, as their clients have adopted technology lawyers have too — although usually lagging well behind. Law firms are slow at adopting technology for at least two reasons. First is the conservative nature of most lawyers who tend to distrust the new. (This tendency has sometimes actually served them well in this area; law firms have typically not been on the "bleeding edge," a term applied to those who adopt technology before it fully works as advertised). Second, members of the legal professional class have long considered "keyboard" work as something that secretaries do and lawyers do not. As late as the early 1990s few attorneys had computers on their desks, despite the fact that their primary job is to produce documents, and computers had by then become pretty efficient at doing that.

This has all changed now. For the last four years, the American Bar Association (ABA) has conducted a survey of technology use in the legal profession. These studies indicate that despite a slow start in adopting technology, they have nearly caught up. The 2006 report noted for example that

---

[44] *See* Eaton, *supra* note 10.

[45] Peter Lattman, *Stanford's Larry Kramer: The State of Our Profession is Bad*, WALL ST.J. LAW BLOG, Oct. 22, 2007, *available at*: www.law.stanford.edu/news/details/1216.

82 percent of law firms now offer laptops to their attorneys, and PDA use had jumped from 23 percent to 35 percent in the prior year.[46] The same report revealed that online research at law firms jumped from 72 percent to 86 percent also in a single year. A related statistic reveals that the use of print research has been slowly shrinking from 80 percent of law firm in 2004, but dropped in the 2006 survey to 58 percent.[47]

As recently as 2006, 85 percent of attorneys had computers in their office, now nearly 100 percent do.[48] E-mail usage is also now nearly total. Further, an extraordinary 94.9 percent of attorneys now produce at least some of their own documents using their computers for word processing.[49] In just the last few years attorneys have also become much more connected while still being mobile through their use of technology while on the road. In 2006, only 69 percent of attorneys used a computer for law-related tasks while away from the office;[50] now 93.6 percent do.[51]

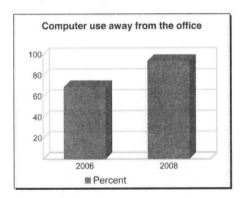

---

[46] MOBILE REPORT 2008, *supra* note 7, at 23.

[47] *Id.*

[48] MOBILE REPORT 2006, *supra* note 7, at 23; MOBILE REPORT 2008, *supra* note 7, at 23.

[49] MOBILE REPORT 2006, *supra* note 7, at 23.

[50] *Id.*

[51] *Id.*

Like nearly everyone else in business today, attorneys find themselves regularly accessing the Internet from home for work-related tasks — in 2008 90.3 percent indicated that they regularly do so and 6.7 percent do so occasionally. The use of smartphones such as Blackberrys has also increased dramatically in just the last few years. In the ABA Technology survey for 2004–2005, only 10 percent of attorneys used smartphones. That percentage increased to 20 percent in the 2006 report, and in the 2008 report had jumped to 66%.

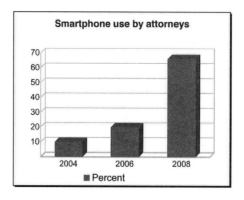

The last decade has also seen the dramatic rise of electronic filing of documents in courts around the country. For a time, many judges resisted it but paper filing is becoming rare. The 2006 ABA survey reported that the percentage of firms that had never e-filed a court document had dropped precipitously from 70 percent to 42 percent. Now more and more courts actually require e-filing, including all Federal district courts and bankruptcy courts, six Federal circuit courts of appeals, and a number of state court systems. It is only a matter of time until paper filing of documents in all courts around the country will be extinct. In many law offices the task of e-filing is often completed by paralegals or secretaries. Still the responsibility lies with the attorney making the filing, so electronic filing remains something that all attorneys need to be able to work with and understand.

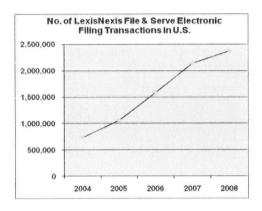

While attorneys may have resisted it for a long time — and lagged behind the business world in the adoption of technology — today, they are as fully connected as their business clients. In short, technology has finally become an ineluctable part of the practice of law. Unfortunately, law schools typically do little or nothing to make sure that their graduates are smart and capable users of all of the myriad forms of technology that are available to help them be effective and connected attorneys.

The Rise of Online Research

For at least 200 years, legal research was conducted exclusively in books. That started to change in the early 1980s. At first it was just one Lexis machine in the law library. Over the next 20 years, Lexis and Westlaw migrated to the desktop and the decline in book research began. Over the last decade, law school libraries all over the country have started to downsize their book collections in favor of online resources. Law firms have followed suit. In a 2007 study of law firms in the Chicago area, Professor Sanford Greenberg at Chicago-Kent Law School found that the ascendancy of online research over print is now beyond debate. His study covered a broad mix of attorneys in different types of law offices, practice areas and sizes of law firms. Greenberg wrote, "When asked to identify their own primary research sources, our respondents overwhelmingly reported that they are more

likely to use online rather than print sources."[52] His study
found that more than two-thirds of the survey respondents go
to online research sources first, while only 13.8 percent
consult print resources first.[53]

Print research is not gone, but it does seem to be fading.
The ABA 2003 technology survey reported that 75 percent of
attorneys regularly used print for their research, but that
figure had shrunk to 58 percent in 2006, 54 percent in the
2004–2005 survey, and in the 2008 survey stood at
52.5 percent.

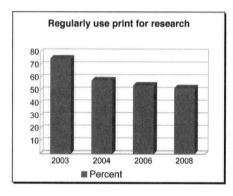

In the 2008 survey, 34.2 percent of the respondents to
the ABA survey reported that they "never" used a physical law
library.[54] Perhaps most revealingly, attorneys very rarely use
print when they are searching for their own state's case law or
for legal forms. In 2006, only 20 percent of the ABA
respondents used print sources to find legal forms, and
that figure shrank to 18.6 percent in the 2008 survey. Today,
95.7 percent of attorneys indicated that they conduct legal
research online in some form.

This is one area in which law schools have done a
reasonably good job, at least in recognizing the need to
prepare students for a world of primarily online research. For
the last 15 years or so, most first year legal research and

---

[52] Sanford N. Greenberg, *Legal Research Training: Preparing Students for a Rapidly Changing Research Environment*, 13 J. LEGAL WRITING 241, 247 (2007).

[53] *Id.* at 248.

[54] LEGAL TECH RES. CTR. (2008), *supra* note 7, at 23.

writing courses have exposed their students to online research. At first they held it off to the spring semester and some schools still do this. But increasingly online research and book research have been integrated. Unfortunately, beyond the first year very little instruction is available in most law schools that teach students how to develop advanced skills in the use of online research, other than what is provided by the commercial, fee-based online services LexisNexis and Westlaw.

Another area where law schools have not done very well is in teaching students to use the increasing number of reliable and free Internet-based legal research resources. With each passing year these resources increase in number and it becomes more imperative for us to teach them because many practicing lawyers are using these sorts of resources already. Professor Greenberg noted that nearly 60 percent of his survey respondents used free web legal research at least occasionally and the 2006 ABA survey put the number even higher, at 72 percent. That total climbed to 88.9 percent in the 2008 ABA report. These numbers indicate not only that increasing amounts of legal materials are becoming available for free on the Internet, but also that attorneys are increasingly finding them reliable and useful.

An interesting, and related, development is the increasing use of Internet citations in judicial opinions. Professor Ellie Margolis of Temple Law School is conducting research in this area. She has found that while in all the U.S. Supreme Court opinions issued in 1996 there was only one Internet citation, by 2003 that number had grown to 14, and by 2008 it had reached 27.[55] This trend, while small, is even more pronounced among the opinions handed down by the Federal circuit courts. The 9th Circuit, for example, has cited in published opinions an Internet-based resource 435 times, and the 7th Circuit 233 times. Not all circuit courts cite the Internet this often. The 4th Circuit has only cited online sources 67 times, the 8th Circuit 78 times. But eight of 13 circuit courts have cited the Internet more than 100 times.[56]

---

[55] Ellie Margolis, Presentation at LWI Biennial Conference, Indianapolis, Indiana, July 15, 2008.

[56] Id.

While librarians (and many others) have looked askance at Wikipedia as a reliable resource, it should be noted that by mid-2008 Wikipedia had been cited in 51 published court cases. Sometimes this was only for a "dictionary" type of cite, or a citation to popular culture that related to the case at hand. But if court opinions are starting to use Wikipedia as a source (for any purpose) it is further evidence that the world of what is considered authoritative to a judge is expanding.

As Professor Margolis has pointed out, this has important implications for legal education. We need to understand, and teach our students about, the changing nature of legal authority.[57] In the past the process of legal research was about finding the right cases, statutes and regulations that applied to a particular client's problem, and this process was fairly routine and contained. Now the net has to be cast much wider and our students need to understand how to do that, and most importantly what to do with what they find.

The Rise of Electronic Discovery

For many years, in both Federal courts and most state trial courts more than 90 percent of cases filed never reached trial. They were either dismissed or a settlement was reached between the parties. In the last decade the number of cases settled before trial in the federal district courts has risen to 98 percent. This phenomenon has been called the "vanishing trial." As a result of this trend, and the trend towards more complex cases (especially in federal courts) the discovery period in litigation has become the make or break time. It is now primarily in discovery that most cases are won or lost.

This is not entirely a bad thing. Court resources are scarce and judges encourage litigants to settle their differences rather than go through complex and costly trials. As long as you believe that both sides are able to glean what they need to know about the merits of each other's case and can reach an equitable settlement as a result of that shared knowledge, then settlements before trial are an important

---

[57] Ellie Margolis, SURFIN' SAFARI — WHY COMPETENT LAWYERS SHOULD RESEARCH ON THE WEB, 10 YALE J. L. & TECH. 82 (2007).

good for society. But the integrity of the discovery process is essential to the healthy functioning of the civil court system.

There have long been debates about how effective the discovery system actually is, because the system largely depends on both parties acting in good faith. Often, though, trust breaks down and neither party is completely innocent of discovery abuses large and small. In the end, clients often get charged for a lot of legal work on minor discovery disputes, few of which advance the clients interests significantly. Despite these opportunities for abuse the discovery system has generally worked well in that it eventually gets both parties to a point where they feel they can reasonably settle the case. If this were not true the number of settlements over the last 30 years would likely have decreased, not increased. Unfortunately the delicate balance in discovery is under serious threat from the addition and complexity presented by the exploding field of electronic discovery.

As recently as ten years ago, when in a litigation, in response to a Rule 34 Request for Production of Documents, paper copies were filed in large boxes and delivered physically by courier to the offices of the attorney who had requested them on behalf of his or her client. Sometimes these productions could be quite large and cumbersome, but the important thing is that they were almost entirely delivered in paper form. Although not exclusively: for at least 25 years it has been possible to obtain items in discovery that were electronic in nature. The discovery rules broadly defined what a "document" was and it was long interpreted to include electronic documents such as diagrams, video tapes and scanned X-rays. So, occasionally, those boxes of paper documents might also include a tape, or, more recently, a CD with electronic information on it.

But increasingly over the last decade companies and individuals have been generating many more documents electronically than ever before. This is, of course, because of the advance of the Internet and especially the expanding use of electronic mail and cell phones, and the ability of these electronic media to capture and retain information. Today it is estimated that 99 percent of the world's information is generated electronically and never takes paper form.[58] Most of these electronic documents contain "metadata," which can either be a simple date and time stamp, or "bread crumbs" that might show who worked on the document and the changes they made to it. A litigation attorney today who produces electronic documents but does not understand metadata is potentially committing malpractice. Not surprisingly, these developments have had a profound effect on civil discovery.

It has been estimated that "a midsized case can generate up to 500 gigabytes of potentially relevant data. It could cost as much as $3.5 million to process and review that much information before production."[59] The problem created by this sheer volume and the attendant complexity is that what is now possible in electronic discovery may simply overwhelm the value of the case to either party. In December, 2006, several new provisions were added to the Federal Rules of Civil Procedure to try to address this concern.

There is currently some confusion, however, in the developing law of what these rules mean as applied to particular litigations and electronic records. There have been over the last few years significant sanctions granted in major litigations caused by electronic discovery missteps by attorneys. Judges have been so convinced that litigants have used eDiscovery to be less than forthcoming when ordered to produce — or have simply made spoliation mistakes — that they have switched the burden of proof,[60] waived the attorney-client privilege[61] or the work product doctrine[62] or imposed severe sanctions on the attorneys involved.[63]

---

[58] Inst. for the Advancement of the Am. Legal Sys. at the Univ. of Denver, Electronic Discovery: A View from the Front Lines 10 (2008).

[59] *Id.* at 4.

[60] Coleman Holdings, Inc. v. Morgan Stanley & Co., No. 502003CA005045X-XOCAI, 2005 WL 679071 (Fla. Cir. Ct. 2005).

[61] Victor Stanley, Inc. v. Creative Pipe, Inc., 250 F.R.D. 251 (Dist. Md. 2008).

[62] Advanced Micro Devices, Inc. v. Intel Corp. (In re Intel Corp. Microprocessor Antitrust Litig.), 2008 U.S. Dist. LEXIS 43920 (D. Del. June 4, 2008).

[63] Qualcomm Inc. v. Broadcom Corp., No. 05cv1958-B (BLM). 2008 U.S. Dist. LEXIS 16897 (S.D. Cal. Mar. 5, 2008).

While the legal aspects of these developments call upon skills that are very much the sorts of things law schools teach well, the electronic aspects are completely new, and very little attempt has been made to address such things in law courses. Indeed, it has been said that eDiscovery "equates to perhaps the biggest new skill set ever thrust upon the profession."[64] This is just one example of how law schools have failed to prepare their graduates for an increasingly important technology-driven aspect of practicing law, especially for a student interested in becoming a litigator.

Another example is one that is related to eDiscovery, but that also has implications for many disciplines other than litigation. It is the rise of large data sets. As technology enables the gathering and sifting of large amounts of electronic information, many disciplines of law will be affected. In a divorce there may be large amounts of data from a home computer involved. In a merger of two large companies there will undoubtedly be massive amounts of competitive business information involved. Lawyers have always been communicators, and a large part of what law school teaches is the traditional rhetoric of the law. But working with and explaining large data sets is a communication skill law schools as yet make no effort to teach. This becomes yet another form of digital literacy that we must help our students master before they graduate.

The Rise of Outsourcing

Another startling trend in the legal profession over the last five years is the rise of outsourcing of what used to be considered attorney work, particularly overseas. Like many of the other changes in the legal profession discussed in this chapter, this has been largely enabled by technology, most especially the growth of the Internet and the installation of trans-Atlantic fiber optic cables. Probably the largest beneficiary of this trend has been the various, and expanding, outsourcing law firms located in India. At first law

---

[64] George L. Paul & Jason R. Baron, INFORMATION INFLATION: CAN THE LEGAL SYSTEM ADAPT? 13 RICH. J.L. & TECH. 10 at *6, Spring 2007.

firm outsourcing was limited to "back office" functions, such as accounting and tech support. But increasingly legal work — which in the past was done by associates in the law firm — has been outsourced overseas.

There are some dire predictions about how significant this trend will be, but at least one suggests that nearly 500,000 U.S. legal jobs will move overseas.[65] Already many in-house legal departments for large American companies such as General Electric have their own legal department "branches" in India. In the past, this work would have been done by attorneys in their own legal department or handled by attorneys in U.S. law firms.

An article in the ACC Docket in 2004, under the Technology and Law Department Management column, touted the benefits of outsourcing legal work to India.[66] Among the projects that it recommended be considered for outsourcing were low-skill tasks such as indexing and coding documents for litigation, or legal transcription, which are rarely done by attorneys in U.S. law firms. The article also recommended that some tasks usually performed by attorneys could be handled competently by attorneys in India such as "fifty-state surveys ... drafting contracts, research memoranda, pleadings and briefs." Those latter tasks are exactly the sorts of things that law schools train their students to do. If they are not going to be doing those things because they have moved off shore — or at least doing them far less — it would be wise for legal educators to be concerned with what they *will* be doing.

Another threat to the delivery of legal services by lawyers based in the U.S. is those legal services that many members of the public are getting for themselves. It is increasingly possible, with the help of books and Internet resources, for members of the general public to prepare their own wills or prepare and file simple incorporation papers, or even file patent applications.[67] Both this trend and the outsourcing

---

[65] Neal St. Anthony, *Outsourcing Hits Legal Services*, STAR TRIB., Jan. 16, 2004, at 1D.

[66] Zachary J. Bossenbroek & Puneet Moheyz, SHOULD YOUR LEGAL DEPARTMENT JOIN THE INDIA OUTSOURCING CRAZE?, ACC Docket, Oct. 2004, at 46.

[67] *See generally* www.nolopress.com.

trend suggest that much of the "lower order" legal tasks will be less and less available to the newly minted graduates of our law schools. If true, this means that in the future a significant number of U.S. Lawyers — graduates of our law schools — will be engaged, earlier in their careers than ever before, in higher order legal tasks. Among these might be management of teams of attorneys in India, or taking on greater responsibility with the client, and doing that sooner than has been typical. Young lawyers may be also called upon to manage large data sets in complex transactions, or in litigations involving significant electronic discovery. It is unclear which aspects of these skills we are teaching, or even contemplating teaching, in our law schools today. With a few bright exceptions, in many ways we are too often preparing the students of today for a law practice of the past.

Further Reading

Laura Owen, *The Tech Evolution: Change or Die*, LAW TECH. NEWS, Jan. 4, 2005.

Rick B. Allen, *Lawyers: Are We a Profession in Distress?*, NEB. LAW., Oct. 1998, at 22.

LEGAL TECH. RES. CTR., AM. BAR ASS'N, 2008 AMERICAN BAR ASSOCIATION LEGAL TECHNOLOGY RESOURCE CENTER SURVEY REPORT: MOBILE LAWYERS TREND REPORT (2008).

Chapter 5

THE CRITICISM OF LEGAL EDUCATION

Considering the amount of significant criticism that has been aimed at legal education over the years the fact that so little has changed is truly extraordinary. Further, since the focus of the criticism has remained remarkably unchanged no matter which person or what entity is speaking, it seems likely that the nature of the criticism is fundamentally sound. It also seems likely that something has made law schools stubbornly resistant to altering their ways — and that this something else has deep and strong roots, and that there are long-standing reasons for its existence.

In fact, this is true. Most law schools draw their academic legitimacy from being parts of larger universities. The academic model therefore will always tend to hold sway. And the academic model simply does not have the same values as the values championed by the critics of legal education. What universities prize most is scholarship. Scholarship requires by its very nature some distance from the day-to-day grind of law practice. A scholar is called upon to look at the forest, not the trees. The practicing lawyer is paid by the hour to work with trees, and rarely has time to look at the forest.

The legal scholar plays a significant and important role in the development of the law. To be sure, there are criticisms about the relevance of some legal scholarship.[68] But on balance, our system of law would suffer if there were no one looking at the big picture — at a scholarly remove — and providing commentary and prescriptions for improvement.

But the skills that academics need and prize are quite different from the skills needed for practicing law. Working lawyers need to think of the specifics of the law as they apply to a particular set of client facts. They rarely have the luxury to worry about the long-term consequences their arguments might have on other clients in other jurisdictions under different sets of facts. Academics need to be able to see and work with broad vistas of the law — across clients, fact patterns and jurisdictions.

This ability to see and work with the theoretical in the law is something the academic world rewards by making those who have it into the elite. In law schools, the best students make the law review and publish most of the majority of legal scholarship that the professors write. Those students often serve as research assistants to law professors, and many go on to judicial clerkships immediately after law school — and often become law professors themselves. Although these students may practice for a year or two at a prestigious firm, it is not considered important, and is certainly not a requirement to join a law faculty where their academic record and their potential as a scholar will be the main consideration. The criticism of legal education has generally been focused on the need for more practical education, and the faculty of law schools — who make the decisions about the law school curriculum — are made of people who are, generally speaking, ill-equipped to teach in this way. Thus, we have a stalemate in legal education, and it is one of the most powerful sources of resistance to change.

---

[68] Adam Liptak, *When Rendering Decisions, Judges are Finding Law Reviews Irrelevant*, N.Y. TIMES, March 19, 2007, at A8; Richard A. Posner, AGAINST THE LAW REVIEWS, LEGAL AFFAIRS, Nov.–Dec. 2004, at 57.

For a long time the explanation offered by academics was that their job was to teach students to "think like a lawyer" and that expecting them to teach the specifics of practicing law would undermine that core responsibility. In other words, the job of a law faculty was to form law students into generalist legal thinkers who could learn the specific requirements of practice either from an apprenticeship program in a law firm, or simply on the ground as they started their legal practice. This view of the role of legal education has dominated for many years.

Of course, part of why it is popular is that it is not wrong, it is just incomplete. Graduating law students do need to be able to "think like a lawyer" — there is no debate about that. They just need to be taught a panoply of other skills as well. Just because that is true (and many seem to agree that it is) there is no reason why this sort of change in legal education has to devalue the traditional academic. But it does mean that more room in the tent will need to be made for other teacher competencies, and more value will need to be conferred on them. In a world of limited resources, this could effectively devalue the traditional academic, but it should not. Indeed, the success of any change depends on it not devaluing the traditional academic. This is fortunately another place where technology can help, by increasing efficiencies and enabling effective pedagogy for skills teaching.

The Criticisms from the Legal Profession

Over the last 30 years members of the legal profession have voiced essentially the same litany of complaints about legal education. Prominent among these complaints are that new law school graduates are not ready for practice, that they do not write well and that they are not sufficiently good at researching the law. Some have also complained that our graduates do not effectively know how to use books for research any more although as more and more practitioners employ online resources successfully, that complaint seems to be waning.

All this criticism is at bottom part of the debate about whether law schools should graduate fully-formed practitioners, or whether they should graduate generalists while the law firms should bear the burden of making them into practitioners. Of course the answer is that law schools should do both. The law schools certainly should and could do better at getting their students ready for practice, although they will never fully fulfill that requirement since there is no way a law school can prepare new lawyers for the specifics of everything they will see in today's varied practices.

But law firms will inevitably need to retain some role in helping new lawyers bridge the gap. Too many senior lawyers abdicate their responsibility to help their young associates, and too many law firms have poor mentoring programs. The bottom line is that law schools should do more and so should law firms. There will always be a gap between law school and law practice. The question is whether law schools should play a larger role in narrowing the gap, and if so, how best to play that role. There has been no shortage of ideas offered in numerous studies and reports dating back nearly 100 years.

The Early Carnegie Reports

The first of these seminal reports on educational method was the 1910 Carnegie Foundation study of medical education primarily authored by the well-known American educator Abraham Flexner.[69] Flexner's report made a tremendous impact on medical education. Until that time there were too many medical schools of questionable quality with inadequate curricula and facilities. Flexner advocated that medical education should have a sound scientific foundation of course, but that this needed to be supplemented by a clinical curriculum that would take place in teaching hospitals. While some of these reforms were already under way in 1910, the Flexner study gets much of the credit for changing the face of medical education. Today, Flexner's model of clinical experience and internships is in force in nearly all medical schools worldwide.

The impact of the Flexner report encouraged the Carnegie Foundation to conduct a similar study of legal education. With the approval of the American Bar Association, they

---

[69] ABRAHAM FLEXNER, MEDICAL EDUCATION IN THE UNITED STATES AND CANADA: A REPORT TO THE CARNEGIE FOUNDATION FOR THE ADVANCEMENT OF TEACHING (1910).

appointed Joseph Redlich, an Austrian law professor, to conduct the study and issue a report. In 1913 he visited 10 law schools over two months and issued his report in 1914.[70]

The Redlich report, like the much later Carnegie Report of 2007, praised the case method, developed in 1871 by Harvard Law School Dean Christopher Columbus Langdell. The Redlich report supported the case method as being a good way to "train the legal mind" because the student is "doing ... what he will be doing as a lawyer."[71] Indeed, the Redlich report states that the use of the case method is dictated by the fact that it is rooted in "the very nature of the common law."[72] But while praising casebooks Redlich also recognized that practical legal education was important and he emphasized strongly the need to use the case method in a more holistic and practical way.

This latter recommendation of the Redlich report had almost no effect, so in the 1920s, the Carnegie Foundation commissioned the Reed report, hoping it would have more influence on legal education. At that time, legal education was available in essentially two forms: the Langdell model prevailed at the academic law schools that were a part of large universities, and the more practice-oriented approach available in smaller schools and informal training programs. The Reed report recommended that more practical skills training be provided in the academic law schools as well. Unfortunately, the 1921 Reed report "created a firestorm" in the ABA[73] partly because of this recommendation, but also because Reed advocated the continuation of these two forms of legal education. The leaders of the ABA at the time argued in favor of one standardized form of legal education, and the Langdell model in the university setting won out. While the alternative schools faded, the number of university-based law schools, and more recently, stand-alone law schools, increased dramatically. But to establish their bona-fides,

---

[70] JOSEF REDLICH, THE COMMON LAW AND THE CASE METHOD IN AMERICAN UNIVERSITY LAW SCHOOLS: A REPORT TO THE CARNEGIE FOUNDATION FOR THE ADVANCEMENT OF TEACHING, BULLETIN NO.8 (1914).

[71] Id. at 23.

[72] Id. at 37.

[73] CARNEGIE 2007, supra note 14, at 44.

these schools typically adopted the Langdell case method-driven curricular format of the schools that they emulated.

The Cramton Report

In the late 1970s, the ABA Section of Legal Education and Admissions to the Bar asked Roger Cramton, the Dean of Cornell Law School, to chair a group of prominent lawyers, judges, and law professors to look at the question of how well law schools were doing in preparing its graduates for practice. The Cramton Report was issued in 1979[74] and this report concurred with some of what the Reed report contained. It recognized the benefit of diversity and experimentation among law schools since a more diverse group of schools would be more likely to prepare their graduates for an increasingly diverse profession. It contained 28 recommendations, many of which recommended that more focus be placed on teaching practice-oriented skills. For example, it urged the increase of teaching "fundamental skills critical to lawyer competence," and cited the need for smaller classes, lower student-faculty ratios and more feedback than just one final exam. Recommendation 12 was: "Law schools and law faculty members should give more attention to what courts, lawmakers, and lawyers do, and how they do it, [and] how the relevant skills are learned...".[75] While there was some increase in clinical education programs in the years following the Cramton report, little else changed.

The MacCrate Report

About 10 years later the ABA Legal Education Committee took another run at the problem by appointing a task force of legal luminaries to produce a further report. The chairman was Robert MacCrate, a prominent New York lawyer, and in 1992 his "Task Force on Law Schools and the Professsion: Narrowing the Gap" issued a study entitled "Legal Education and Professional Development — An Educational Conti-

---

[74] ABA TASK FORCE ON LAWYER COMPETENCY, REPORT AND RECOMMENDATIONS: THE ROLE OF LAW SCHOOLS (1979).

[75] *Id.* at 5.

nuum."[76] The MacCrate Report urged that law schools focus on teaching ten fundamental and highly practical lawyering skills. Among these were problem solving, legal analysis, legal research, counseling, negotiation, and organization and management of legal work. It also recommended that law schools focus on teaching several fundamental values of the profession such as providing competent representation, striving to promote justice and improving the profession.

> MacCrate Fundamental Lawyering Skills
> - Problem Solving
> - Legal Analysis and Reasoning
> - Legal Research
> - Factual Investigation
> - Communication
> - Counseling
> - Negotiation
> - Litigation and ADR Procedures
> - Organization and Management of Legal Work
> - Recognizing and Resolving Ethical Dilemmas
>
> MacCrate Fundamental Values of the Profession
> - Provision of Competent Representation
> - Striving to Promote Justice, Fairness, and Morality
> - Striving to Improve the Profession
> - Professional Self-Development

In the period following the issuance of the MacCrate report, there was some considerable discussion of its recommendations, such as at the annual AALS conferences. However, since the report originated with the ABA, and so was perceived as coming from the practicing bar, it was resisted by the legal academy. In addition, even though the report recommended a significant increase in the teaching of practical skills, the ABA did not adjust its accreditation standards to require that all law students take such courses. The report also urged that bar examiners test competency in these sorts of skills, but few state boards of bar examiners have moved to make such changes. While much discussion was engendered by the MacCrate report, and there was

---

[76] AM. BAR ASS'N SECTION OF LEGAL EDU. AND ADMISSIONS TO THE BAR, LEGAL EDUCATION AND PROFESSIONAL DEVELOPMENT — AN EDUCATIONAL CONTINUUM: REPORT OF THE TASK FORCE ON LAW SCHOOLS AND THE PROFESSION: NARROWING THE GAP (1992) [hereinafter MACCRATE REPORT].

another modest increase in clinical programs, legal education successfully resisted significant change again.[77]

The Mertz Report

Yet three more reports were issued in 2007 that offered criticisms of legal education and made suggestions for improvement. The first of these was a linguistic study of law schools by Elizabeth Mertz, a senior Research Fellow at the American Bar Foundation. In her book, *The Language of Law School — Learning to Think Like a Lawyer*, Professor Mertz studied actual classroom discussions at eight law schools of varying status around the country. What she found was that the case method is a closed linguistic form which — because of the heavy emphasis it places on abstract legal authority — acts to separate the law from the complex social and human interactions leading to actual cases, and which law students also need to appreciate as part of their learning.

While Professor Mertz was not in favor of dispensing completely with the case method — since lawyers need to know the linguistic aspects of the law to function as attorneys — she recommended greater emphasis on "moral judgment and fully contextualized consideration of human conflict."[78] She urged that law professors be more cognizant to the limitations of the case method, and that they bring such appreciation into the classroom. Over the years there have been many criticisms of the political leanings and limitations of the law school curriculum, but few that have taken such a broad empirical and linguistic approach to this criticism as Professor Mertz.

The Carnegie Report of 2007

Another of the 2007 reports was issued by the Carnegie Foundation for the Advancement of Teaching, which once again examined the state of legal education.[79] This effort,

---

[77] John O. Sonsteng et al., LEGAL EDUCATION: A PRACTICAL APPROACH FOR THE TWENTY-FIRST CENTURY, 34 WM. MITCHELL L. REV. 303, 370 (2007).

[78] ELIZABETH MERTZ, THE LANGUAGE OF LAW SCHOOL — LEARNING TO THINK LIKE A LAWYER 220 (2007).

[79] CARNEGIE 2007, *supra* note 14.

entitled *Educating Lawyers: Preparation for the Profession of Law*, was part of a larger group of studies conducted by the Foundation of several forms of professional education, called the Preparation for the Professions Program that included investigations of schools of divinity, nursing and engineering. The primary author of the report, William Sullivan, had previously written another broad study of the various forms of professional education in America.[80]

Sullivan's report noted that legal education has long been surprisingly successful in rapidly inculcating the methods of legal analysis and "thinking like a lawyer." The study attributed this to the success of the case method, which the report called the "signature pedagogy" of law school. But Sullivan also noted that while the case method has strengths, it also has consequences, among them those noted by Professor Mertz, and including its disconnection from practical contextual learning.

Sullivan's report also identified what it called "the three apprenticeships" that aspiring lawyers must experience: 1) the cognitive apprenticeship — the traditional learning to "think like a lawyer," 2) the skills apprenticeship — the newer efforts to teach students to "do like a lawyer," and 3) the professional formation apprenticeship — the still newer concept that law students need explicit and pervasive instruction in developing a "professional identity and purpose." The report asserted that "law schools need to do a better job integrating the teaching of legal doctrine with a much stronger focus on helping students develop practical 'lawyering' skills and understandings of ethical and moral considerations."

> **The Three Apprenticeships**
>
> - The Cognitive Apprenticeship – "Think like a lawyer"
>
> - The Skills Apprenticeship – "Do like a lawyer"
>
> - The Professional Formation Apprenticeship – Develop a "professional identity and purpose"

---

[80] WILLIAM M. SULLIVAN, WORK AND INTEGRITY: THE CRISIS AND PROMISE OF PROFESSIONALISM IN AMERICA (2004).

In short, the 2007 Carnegie report recommended that legal education should move toward a more "theory in context" approach, and that it should join legal ethics with nearly every facet of the three year curriculum. It also noted, with considerable disapproval, that students do not receive enough feedback from their teachers and urged significant changes in assessment of student work. In other words, while praising many things that are good about legal education, it prescribed a more practice-oriented approach that generally speaking, would require a lower faculty-student ratio than is common in law schools. It made little in the way of recommendations about how to make these sorts of significant changes in legal education happen. And it did not at all address how much money it would cost to follow its precepts.

It is odd and troubling that this much anticipated report makes only one reference to technology in teaching (when mentioning in passing that occasionally law teachers use PowerPoint.)[81] The earlier studies of legal education were written before the advent of computers and the Internet — and thus before the influence that both have had on the legal profession — so naturally they made no mention of it. But the omission in the 2007 Carnegie report of the uses of technology in law schools and in the legal profession strikes one as quite odd. So does the failure to mention how technology could help address some of the concerns it raises. In this respect, the Carnegie Report of 2007 might just as well have been written in 1994 when public use of the Internet was just getting started.

The CLEA Report

In the same year as the recent Carnegie Report, the Clinical Legal Education Association (CLEA) issued a report entitled "Best Practices for Legal Education."[82] This study is more direct it its indictment of the failures of law schools, and

---

[81] *Id.* at 50.

[82] Roy Stuckey et al., Best Practices for Legal Education (2007).

clearer in its suggested solutions. It starts by putting a frame on legal education that has, essentially, never been in place before, or certainly not at most law schools. It suggests that all law schools should start by setting goals and end by assessing how they are doing at achieving those goals, and that this frame should be built and remain in place at all law schools. This alone is a radical notion, since few law schools ever engage in any such programs of carefully constructed self-examination.

The CLEA report follows by making several recommendations for improving what happens inside the frame of goal setting and assessment. It sets out clear instructions for upgrading the quality of instruction generally, and mandates that the program of instruction be designed to meet the goals that have been set by the institution. The report strongly favors what it calls "experiential learning," which although specifically a call for more clinical education, can be thought of more broadly as a recommendation in favor of teaching legal theory in the context of practice.

Unlike the 2007 Carnegie report, the CLEA study does mention the role that technology can play in improving the quality of instruction in law school. "[I]f technology is not the future of legal education," it notes, "it is at least a part of the future."[83] Although giving only two pages to the subject, the report points out that "current technologies allow law professors to implement many of the best practices described in this document."[84] It also notes that technology can enable teachers to assess their students' performance more often and better interact with them generally, a recommendation that runs throughout the report.

The Law School Survey of Student Engagement

These many examinations and criticisms of legal education over the last 100 years have, for the most part, largely ignored the persons most affected — our students. This omission began to be addressed in 2003 by the expansion to law schools of the National Survey of Student Engagement,

---

[83] *Id.* at 159.

[84] *Id.* at 160.

administered by the Center for Postsecondary Research at the University of Indiana. Over the next five years, the Law School Survey of Student Engagement (LSSSE) was administered at 148 law schools, and more than 100,000 law students responded to the survey. The LSSSE has sought to measure the level of engagement by law students in their studies because it is generally accepted by all educators that students who are interested and engaged are more likely to learn and more importantly, to better retain what they learn over time.

What our students have said through the LSSSE about their legal education is troubling. In the 2004 report, a third of respondents said they never discussed ideas from class or from their readings with a professor outside of class. In the 2005 report, 40 percent of respondents noted that they never participated in co-curricular activities, such as journals or moot court. In the 2006 report, 24 percent of 2L students indicated that they never received prompt feedback from their professors. In the 2007 survey, nearly a quarter of 3Ls indicated that they often or very often went to class unprepared.

That last number — the percentage of 3L students who regularly come to class unprepared — has hovered around 20–25 percent over the five years of the administration of the LSSSE. When 3L students come to class unprepared to learn, they are indicating in a strong way their lack of engagement with what is going on. It seems a substantial percentage of our third year students are voting with their feet and with their time and they are simply no longer fully engaged in the educational enterprise. This is particularly troubling since the third year is when students should be most engaged in preparing for practice, making the transition from law school to work. Perhaps this is the most telling criticism of all on the state of most legal education today. A year when students should be vitally interested hardly engages them at all.

The Rising Cost of Legal Education

Adding point to these critical studies, and doubtless helping give rise to some, is the fact that law school tuitions have been rising exponentially. Between 1992 and 2003 the cost of living in the United States rose 28 percent. In the same decade tuition at public law schools increased 134 percent for residents and 100 percent for non-residents, and tuition at private law schools increased 76 percent.[85] Today, as one survey summed up, "more than half of law students expect to owe more than $60,000 in law school debt at graduation, and one in five expect to owe more than $120,000."[86] In all, 88 percent of law students have incurred at least some debt to attend law school.[87]

It is no wonder that there has been increasing pressure on schools on the cost factor alone. At the same time, the thrust of most of the criticism is that students need more skills training and other cost-intensive improvements such as lower faculty-student ratios, and increased faculty feedback and interaction with students. These changes — if made on anything but a small scale — will further increase costs when there is very little leeway to do so. Large scale changes of this kind could blow the roof off law school budgets and send tuitions higher still. It seems to be a Catch 22, a worrisome change/cost conundrum that law schools will be hard pressed to resolve. There may be a way out, though, mainly through better and more inventive uses of technology.

The Humanizing Movement

In exchange for the high cost of legal education that we charge our students, a growing body of sentiment and research suggests that we may not just be educating our students in a less than effective fashion, but that we may actually be causing them harm. Further, this view posits that we may also be causing harm to the legal profession in the way we prepare our students for practice. This view of legal education suggests not just that our students may be insufficiently prepared to practice law, but that they may be insufficiently prepared to live the life of a lawyer. Numerous studies have noted that law students are depressed and anxious at rates higher than students studying in other

---

[85] William K. S. Wang, FOURTH PANEL: NEW DEALS: THE RESTRUCTURING OF LEGAL EDUCATION ALONG FUNCTIONAL LINES, 17 J. CONTEMP LEGAL ISSUES 331, 333 (2008)

[86] LAW SCH. SURVEY OF STUDENT ENGAGEMENT CTR. FOR POSTSECONDARY RESEARCH, 2008 LAW SCHOOL SURVEY OF STUDENT ENGAGEMENT, Overview at 4 (2008).

[87] Id.

graduate disciplines. According to one such study, "law students almost always reported higher levels of anxiety than comparison groups, including medical students. In some cases they report mean scores on anxiety measures that are comparable to psychiatric populations."[88] Efforts to research and investigate the forms and causes of this problem have come to be known as the "humanizing movement" and a group of interested members of the movement recently received section status in the American Association of Law Schools under the name of "Balance in Legal Education."

This group focuses much of its most severe criticism on the "breaking down" process that has long been a part of legal education — the so-called "Kingsfield" approach that involves humiliation of the student through an authority-based, top-down attitude in the classroom. Instead, the humanizing movement supports a broad range of changes that are needed across legal education such as working to increase a sense of relatedness in our students, building up their sense of competency, and fostering their individual values — generally, to provide what is known in psychological circles as "autonomy support."

In addition, the humanizers are concerned that the typical law school in teaching students to think like a lawyer effectively separates them from their moral values, disconnecting them from a fundamental sense of right and wrong. Worse, law schools send a message that this is the norm in the practice of law. It may be, these critics suggest, that law school is where new lawyers learn that what is right or wrong is defined by what you can or cannot get away with.

Further, the humanizers maintain that in turning our students into small information silos — with the only assessment being a solo performance on a final exam — we lose opportunities to teach them in ways that foster community and a sense of relatedness. If we break down the student's sense of competency, we likely cause more damage than benefit, and perhaps instill not only anxiety in the short term, but insecurity in practice for the long term. If we treat them as interchangeable widgets, we run the risk of

---

[88] Matthew M. Dammeyer & Narina Nunez, CURRENT KNOWLEDGE AND FUTURE DIRECTIONS, 23 LAW & HUM. BEHAV. 55, 61 (1999).

encouraging their disengagement and cynicism about what they are engaged in doing in law school and beyond.

Larry Krieger, a clinical professor at Florida State University law school, has conducted pioneering research on these questions. A longitudinal study he conducted with Ken Sheldon, professor of psychology at the University of Missouri, showed that it does not take long for us to break down our students. Most young college graduates entering law schools, they found, showed a healthy sense of well being, intact values and strong motivation.[89] But after only six months in law school the values, motivation and well-being of the students showed marked decreases and there were increases in depression and even symptoms of physical ills.[90] Krieger has noted, "these changes predict continuing decreases in life satisfaction and happiness, and they are fully consistent with the reports of distress, dissatisfaction, and loss of ethics and values among practicing lawyers."[91]

In a more recent study, Krieger and Sheldon looked at the effects of varying "autonomy support" among students at two different law schools. Autonomy support is a psychological term that is part of self determination theory, which posits that "when authorities provide 'autonomy support' and acknowledge their subordinates' initiative and self-directedness, those subordinates discover, retain and enhance their intrinsic motivations ..."[92]

Krieger and Sheldon have theorized that the autonomy-defeating aspects of much of legal education may be the root cause of the decrease in values, motivation and well-being of law students.[93] The difference between the two law schools in their study was in the emphasis placed on scholarship versus

---

[89] Lawrence S. Krieger, INSTITUTIONAL DENIAL ABOUT THE DARK SIDE OF LAW SCHOOL, AND FRESH EMPIRICAL GUIDANCE FOR CONSTRUCTIVELY BREAKING THE SILENCE, 52 J. LEGAL EDUC. 112, 122 (2002).

[90] Id. 122–23.

[91] Id.

[92] Lawrence S. Krieger & Kennon M. Sheldon, UNDERSTANDING THE NEGATIVE EFFECTS OF LEGAL EDUCATION ON LAW STUDENTS: A LONGITUDINAL TEST AND EXTENSION OF SELF-DETERMINATION THEORY, 33 PERSONALITY & SOC. PSYCHOL. BULL. 883 (2007) [hereinafter Krieger & Sheldon 2007].

[93] Id.

teaching, and specifically practice-focused teaching. The school with the emphasis on scholarship was ranked higher than the school with the greater focus on teaching. The school with the greater focus on teaching, particularly practice teaching, fostered a higher level of autonomy and competence in its students and lower stress levels. In other words, more skills teaching equates to more autonomy support. The striking result of the study was that the school with the higher autonomy support of its students had a higher bar pass rate, even though it was a lower ranked school.[94] The results of their study constitute an indictment of the usual modus operandi at many law schools and confirm what many have long suspected, that we may actually be causing psychological and even physical harm to our students.

So far we have seen how our students are changing, how the practice of law is changing, and how the criticisms of legal education are becoming more forceful and focused. But while the various reports about the problems in legal education essentially all agree, they offer little in terms of resolving the cost issue, and so they all fall short in providing practical solutions. The fact that the more recent ones say very little about the role technology can play in crafting practical solutions to their criticisms is surprising, to say the least, since so much has been happening on that front at the same time.

Further Reading

WILLIAM M. SULLIVAN ET AL., EDUCATING LAWYERS (2007).

ROY STUCKEY ET AL., BEST PRACTICES FOR LEGAL EDUCATION: A VISION AND A ROAD MAP (2007).

AM. BAR ASS'N SECTION OF LEGAL EDU. AND ADMISSIONS TO THE BAR, LEGAL EDUCATION AND PROFESSIONAL DEVELOPMENT — AN EDUCATIONAL CONTINUUM: REPORT OF THE TASK FORCE ON LAW SCHOOLS AND THE PROFESSION: NARROWING THE GAP (1992).

JAMES R. MAXEINER, EDUCATING LAWYERS NOW AND THEN: AN ESSAY COMPARING THE 2007 AND 1914 CARNEGIE FOUNDATION REPORT ON LEGAL EDUCATION (2007).

ELIZABETH MERTZ, THE LANGUAGE OF LAW SCHOOL: LEARNING TO "THINK LIKE A LAWYER" (2007).

---

[94] *Id.*

Chapter 6

THE MARCH OF TECHNOLOGY

Technological development has been with us for centuries, and it is an unstoppable force. Robert Friedel, Professor of The History of Technology at the University of Maryland, maintains that this force comes from the very human need to improve upon what has gone before. Because technology creates change, it is usually resisted, and often ridiculed or mocked. When it succeeds in its primary drive — to improve upon something we currently have — it only does so after being gradually, grudgingly accepted.[95] We often want to blame technology for the added complexity that it brings in our lives. But it is not the fault of technology itself — it is an unstoppable, human, and essentially neutral force.

While Alan Kay said "Technology is anything invented after you were born," one of his colleagues at the Xerox PARC

---

[95] *See generally,* ROBERT FRIEDEL, ZIPPER: AN EXPLORATION OF NOVELTY (1994); ROBERT FRIEDEL, A CULTURE OF IMPROVEMENT: TECHNOLOGY AND THE WESTERN MILLENNIUM (2007).

lab, Danny Hillis, modified that definition: "Technology," he said, "is anything that doesn't work yet." Both are helpful definitions for this chapter because a lot of what we have called "educational technology" has been in a development phase for at least the last 15 years, and for a long time did not strictly "work" yet. When technology does start to "work" for its intended purpose, there is a period when we have to learn about and understand its benefits before we integrate it into our lives and livelihoods. Finally, we stop noticing it and it does not seem like technology any more.

We are not yet at that point with technology in education, and the transition to using it widely and routinely will doubtless take a decade or so more — perhaps longer. Transitions in technology from new, not working and annoying, to accepted, working and invisible, take longer than we expect or realize. In his book *Zipper*, which recounts the colorful history of that invention, Professor Friedel explains how and why it took almost 40 years for the zipper to overcome market resistance and gain broad acceptance. While there are technologies that have found acceptance over shorter periods — Edison's light bulb is an example — the story of the zipper is instructive for those of us interested in the application and use of technology in legal education.

The primary resistance to the zipper came in three phases. First, it did not work particularly well for at least the first 10 years after its invention. Second, it was expensive compared to what it was replacing: very cheap buttons. Third, for a long time after it could be said to "work," and to do so very well, it was resisted because the benefit was not sufficiently understood. These are, roughly, the phases we can expect to see in the broad and deep adoption of technology in the delivery of legal education. While educational technology is finally reaching the point where it can be said to "work," it remains expensive (at least initially), and the benefits are not yet sufficiently understood.

Because the force driving technological development is to improve what came before, we often have the matching expectation that technology will solve everything and lead us to some form of utopia. It usually falls far short of that goal. The zipper was an improvement over buttons, but not that much of one. Today, zippers save us time that we would have to spend fastening things with buttons, but it would not have been the end of the world had zippers never been invented. When we expect too much of technology, hoping for a utopian future, we set ourselves up for disappointment. And when we blame it for not fulfilling what we had in mind, we tend to resist it even more the next time the topic comes around. As the poet Ogden Nash once wrote (in jest): "Progress may have been all right once, but it went on too long."[96]

We must recognize that technology works in granular ways, that is, not the same way for everyone or for every purpose. The zipper, which we now think of as integral to clothing, originally made its inroads into the market through tobacco pouches and galoshes. For this reason, while this chapter will introduce and explain numerous forms of educational technology that can effectively be applied to law schools, it is not intended to be a prescription for every school to follow in its technology plans. Each school will have specific, local requirements that will create different paths to acceptance of greater use of technology in its curriculum, so a uniform plan for each school is unlikely to work.

In understanding better what technology is — and is not — good for, perhaps a useful analogy would be to compare it to a sledgehammer. If you use a sledgehammer at full swing it will break up concrete. But if you use it to drive a brad into soft wood — well, you can use it for that, but you have to hold it up near the head and tap lightly. It is the same with technology applications in education. A laptop is a sledgehammer that can be a window into a very powerful research resource. If used well in the classroom it can contribute very effectively to learning in ways we have never had available before. But if it is used to play solitare, well, you can use it for that, but it is a waste of what it can do. Similarly, if you input a general search into Google for legal resources, you will find some helpful things, but the results will probably not be as good as a more precise search in a customized legal database. With technology it is increasingly our job to teach our students how to use the sledgehammer appropriately — to the benefit of their learning in law school and, when they get into practice, to the benefit of their practice and their clients.

---

[96] THE BEST OF OGDEN NASH 431 (Linell Nash Smith ed., 2007).

The remainder of this chapter offers an assessment of the educational technology tools we have available today and describes, at least generally, their applicability to legal education. It is not meant to be comprehensive in this regard, but rather to show how close we are to the point where technology is finally maturing enough so that it can actually help us be better teachers, and to help our students learn better and be better prepared for the practices they will be joining. Further, it can help us address the change/cost conundrum in legal education.

The Laptop in the Classroom

The first order of business is to address the controversial question of the laptop in the law school classroom. In the last few years there has been considerable discussion and concern among law faculties across the country that the laptop — and the temptation of the Internet — in the classroom is a disruptive influence. The concern is that students are tempted to surf the 'net or check sports scores rather than paying attention sufficiently for the teacher to get a good Socratic discussion going. As a result of these concerns, a number of professors have banned laptops from their classrooms. A few law schools have even shut the Internet off in their classrooms as well.

There is no doubt that laptops in the classroom can become a distraction to students — we all know this. Not so well known is that many students are currently using their laptops in class in ways that are clearly supportive of their learning — without any help from the professors who teach them. If you ask students what they are doing with them in class they will admit to occasionally checking their e-mail and the like. But they will also tell you how, when they have to step out of the classroom to go to the restroom, they will e-mail (or IM) a friend in class, "Hey, what did I miss?" Students who are stuck in the back of large 90-student classrooms where the professor writes in very small script will e-mail fellow students who sit in the front for a translation. Another student will write his notes while the laptop's built-in microphone is capturing the audio of the lecture, which helps connect the two later. Other students will look up a case that a professor mentions but was not in the assigned reading. First year students, who are, of course, learning a new language, often will use their laptops to look up definitions of legal terms that they do not know or do not remember. Still others will use the Internet to research the background on a controversial case that the professor is discussing.[97] These are all, of course, useful and appropriate uses of the laptop in class. If more law professors were aware of these legitimate uses of laptops in class, it seems likely they would be hard pressed to object.

These legitimate uses are compelling in themselves, but if laptops were actually integrated into the teaching and learning methods presented in class by the professor, the benefits of allowing laptops in the classroom would so strongly outweigh the minor distractions they pose that the case in favor would be beyond doubt. Learning to usefully integrate laptops into our classroom pedagogy will take time and will not be easy. Some professors will continue to object that laptops can occasionally be distracting. But banning them or shutting off the Internet is a backward looking approach that would actually impair the learning abilities of students who count on laptops as learning tools. Instead, we have to discover how to leverage them in the classroom, and choose the path of pedagogical growth rather than the path of pedagogical atrophy.

Much of the "evidence" that laptops are "bad" may simply be based on outmoded forms of instruction and assessment in legal education. One area of growth would be in reforming the ways law schools assess student performance. Most forms of assessment in law school — especially the much criticized final exam that determines 100 percent of the grade — amount to little more than exercises in recall and regurgitation. But this is not, as many criticisms have noted, the mode of assessment that we need. Indeed it is one we need to leave behind (or at least reduce).[98] Instead of the old lecture course with its do-or-die final, we need to be moving, as many critics have also said, toward more problem-solving and

---

[97] This information was gathered from a formal, anonymous web-based survey conducted by the author in April, 2007. Results are available at: http://www.lawschool2.org.

[98] CARNEGIE 2007, *supra* note 14, at 166–67.

practice-oriented modes of instruction. Laptops in the class-room, when properly leveraged, can aid professors in making exactly these sorts of shifts, since they provide greater instructional flexibility and support the use of problem-based materials and hands-on learning.

Whether we like it or not, the world is moving at an ever faster pace, and the lawyers of tomorrow will need to be ready for that world. Our students know this and it is partly why they use their laptops in class — it is already second nature to them to use technology to do more in less time. If we ban the laptops our students will never again have a safe place to learn how to use them effectively in the law, and we are sending them into a world that will demand they have this skill.

Some opponents of laptops lament that by having them, students become simply demon typists, madly transcribing rather than listening sufficiently in class and that this is reason enough to ban them. One problem with this criticism is that it assumes all students are the same. It has been established beyond dispute by numbers of studies that students have varied learning styles. For example, some need to type everything, and then need to review their notes after class to achieve the best level of retention. Others take fewer but more selective notes on the laptops — cues, so to speak, that will spark memory later. Still other students prefer to take notes by hand and transcribe them later, using that process to put them in the memory bank.

The problem is not that students are transcribing more than listening. The problem is that we have rarely recognized that we have a responsibility to help our students understand what their learning styles are, and to wisely use technology to support their learning. This is true of all forms of learning, but is especially important in the law. After all, most lawyers do not know the answer to a client's problem when they first hear it. They have to learn the answer and then explain it to the client — and others such as judges, insurance adjusters and opposing counsel. In other words, we should expand our educational mission from simply creating more lawyers to creating life-long learners who are skilled in researching, understanding, and explaining legal concepts quickly and efficiently. Merely lamenting that our students are occasion-ally misusing the laptops — and making no additional effort — is just another form of abdicating our expanding teaching responsibilities.

Some opponents of laptops in the classroom like to cite cognitive research which suggests that multitasking impedes learning.[99] While this research is hardly conclusive, it makes intuitive sense that when we try to do four things it is hard to process each as fully as when we are trying to do only one. But there are several problems with applying the multitasking literature to an argument against laptops. First, it assumes that everything that happens in a law school classroom is essential to learning. While that might be a laudable ideal, it is not the reality. Suppose, for example, a student asks a question to which another student already knows the answer. That second student will just sit there bored — unless he or she has a laptop with which to check something else or work on class notes. This seems like a good use of time, rather than a bad one. That student is still listening, with half an ear, so to speak, to know when the professor has finished the answer and is lecturing again. Second, it assumes that there is no need in life to effectively multitask, or that there might be no such times in the practice of law. Lawyers in fact must often juggle several different inputs at the same time and our graduates need to know how to do this effectively. Third, it assumes that our students do not know how to make decisions about when to multitask and when to focus on one thing. Many law students have developed these coping skills quite well. Fourth, it assumes that we their law professors have no role to play in helping them to know when to multitask and when to focus on one lawyering activity. So to maintain that simply because some research suggests that multitasking can impede learning is at best an incomplete argument against laptops in the classroom and one that also abdicates our responsibilities to our students.

A considerable amount of research has already been conducted on laptops in the classroom at both the high school and undergraduate level. A study conducted in a psychology course at the U.S. Military Academy at West Point found statistically significant improvements in learning in a group

[99] Kevin Yamamoto, BANNING LAPTOPS IN THE CLASSROOM: IS IT WORTH THE HASSLE?, 57 J.LEGAL EDUC. 477 (2007).

of students using laptops in class.[100] Another study conducted in a high school design course with 27 students 17–18 years of age found that the laptop students had higher class participation and learning interest than the 22 non-laptops using students who were also part of the study.[101] More research probably needs to be done, and especially in the law school environment, but it seems quite clear already that the use of laptops in the classroom is not on balance disruptive, but rather can support better learning.

Then there is the issue of supporting the autonomy — the self-esteem and independence — of our students, which Larry Krieger's research strongly says we must do.[102] It is obvious that banning laptops from class would threaten that goal. Students today are so used to communicating through technology and using it in their learning. Banning laptops in class because we do not have confidence that our students can use them wisely would not only undermine their autonomy, it would infantilize them. If we want to teach this generation effectively, we should honor their facility with technology rather than put it off limits. Professors who decide to ban laptops are simply announcing to the world that they want to teach their law school classes the way they always have — before laptops, before the Internet, before cell phones. These teachers are, in effect, announcing to the world that they want to turn the clock back, and continue to be the "Sage on the Stage."

In short, efforts to ban laptops from law school classrooms are short-sighted and counter-productive. The problem is not that we have laptops in the classroom, but that we do not always use them well. Law faculties opened the classrooms to laptops without learning how to leverage them

---

[100] James Efaw et. al, MIRACLE OR MENACE? TEACHING AND LEARNING WITH LAPTOP COMPUTERS IN THE CLASSROOM: A STUDY OF INTEGRATING LAPTOPS INTO CLASSROOM INSTRUCTION FOUND STATISTICALLY SIGNIFICANT IMPROVEMENTS IN STUDENT LEARNING, EDUCAUSE QUARTERLY, Nov. 3, 2004, at 10.

[101] Michael Trimmel & Julia Bachmann, COGNITIVE, SOCIAL, MOTIVATIONAL AND HEALTH ASPECTS OF STUDENTS IN LAPTOP CLASSROOMS, 20 J. COMPUTER ASSISTED LEARNING 151 (2004).

[102] Krieger & Sheldon 2007, *supra* note 92.

effectively. They worry that students are not using them correctly, but do not bother to teach them how to use them effectively. And some have never bothered to change their teaching methods to take advantage of the benefits the technology offers.

Of course, as with everything, there are exceptions. Some law school classes are mainly about thinking — or more precisely, broadening and developing analytical powers. They require professors who are accomplished lecturers, and they require the full attention of the students. Open laptops in that context are generally more of a burden than a benefit. But dealing with the presence of laptops during those sorts of classes is easy. All the teacher needs to do is ask students to shut them. This can make a valuable point, namely that there are times to use them and times not to. The teacher who makes this point will likely get heightened attention from all the students in the room.

But a complete ban on laptops in all classes throughout a law school is today almost unthinkable. Most importantly it would damage the digital literacy our students will need for practice. Law professors or entire faculties considering such a ban should at least postpone it while they take a hard look at their educational goals and consider the digital literacy for practice that their students will need. If they take any responsibility for that form of competency in their graduates they cannot ban laptops. It is as simple as that.

The Educational Technology Maturing Now

Banning laptops now would be particularly unwise and counterproductive because in the last several years, educational technology has matured sufficiently to be truly useful, creating effective new classroom tools. Just five years ago we did not have Wikis, Clickers, Podcasting, and Mindmapping, all of which are now being used broadly in education and increasingly in legal education.

A wiki is a classic Web 2.0 technology — web-based software that supports collaborative writing projects. The most famous wiki, of course, is Wikipedia, the contributor-written encyclopedia that long since exceeded 10 million entries.[103] Wikis are an ideal technology for supporting the sort of collaborative learning many theorists consider should be an integral part of education. They can support educational objectives such as group writing or research projects in a law school class. Wikis allow students to work asynchronously — which also supports their autonomy — and yet together in a collaborative way. Each revision to a project potentially generates learning for the entire group. Examples of the use of a wiki in a law school class would include: 1) a peer edit of a draft excerpt from a brief in a legal writing course, 2) a communally created outline for a casebook course, 3) a group research project in an international law course, 4) a location for shared class notes, or 5) a small group research paper in a seminar class. This technology while relatively new, has already matured to the point where it can be used in creative and effective ways to support the learning, and the autonomy, of our students.

Another highly useful and relatively new technology is the Student Response System, nicknamed "Clickers" because the response units look like television remote controls. Clickers have been employed in education for a number of years. At the undergraduate level they started in science classes such as chemistry and physics.[104] They have mostly been used, and still are, for the administration of quizzes, the system making it possible to publish the results almost immediately. Clicker systems for education are widely available from such vendors as Beyond Question and Turning Point.[105]

The way they work is this: Students are provided with the clickers — or they buy them at the school bookstore — while the teacher plugs a receiver unit into his or her laptop. The receiver unit and the teacher's PowerPoint work in tandem. For a quiz, the teacher's PowerPoint uses slides that project

---

[103] *See* Stacy Schiff, *Know It All — Can Wikipedia Conquer Expertise?*, NEW YORKER, July 31, 2006, *available at* http://www.newyorker.com/archive/2006/07/31/06073/Fa_Fact.

[104] Winnie Hu, *Students Click and a Quiz Becomes a Game*, N.Y. TIMES, Jan. 28, 2008, at B1; Claudia Dreifus, *A Conversation with Carl Weiman — Physics Laureate Hopes to Help Students Over the Science Blahs*, N.Y. TIMES, Nov. 1, 2005, at F2.

[105] http://www.smartoom.com/; http://www.turningtechnologies.com

questions on the screen while students use their clickers to respond.

The benefits of all this in law school teaching can be dramatic. For years critics have hammered the old lecture format for relying too heavily on the regurgitation of case law and for basing a student's entire grade on a single make-or-break final exam. Legal education in general has been criticized for the low level of feedback that students receive. This is where clickers could offer a great deal of help. Responding to this criticism, some professors who teach casebook courses have increasingly been giving midterm examinations and other quizzes. Some of these have consisted of multiple choice questions and so using clickers to administer such tests is a natural. The system not only makes giving the tests more efficient, but also makes it possible to provide students with immediate feedback several times a semester. Other sorts of law school classes besides the lecture courses could also benefit.

Still another form of maturing technology is the podcast. A podcast is simply a form of time-shifting for audio files, much as a VCR used to do with television shows. What makes it a podcast is that the file is in a form that can play on a portable MP3 player such as an iPod. The ubiquity of the iPod has led to the huge growth in podcasting. The growth of the iTunes platform as the center for the posting and downloading of podcasts has supported the explosive growth of this form of distributing content.

Podcasting a class is a fairly simple process and can be supported by the technical departments at most law schools. All that is needed is a method of digitally capturing the content of the class and digital microphones with capture capability are available at most office supply stores for about $100. Purchasing one of these, turning it on and putting it on the podium in the classroom is all that would be required of the professor. The technical department can then make it into a podcast, and post it either to a faculty website, or to iTunes itself. In 2007, Apple launched iTunes U, which supports the posting and distribution of educational podcasts of this sort, which requires even less intervention by the technical support staff of each law school.

The reason to podcast law school classes is simple: it provides yet another form in which students can learn using a technology they are familiar and comfortable with. Many of us already have the technical support at our law schools to tape our law school classes when requested and podcasting is no different, it is just another media form that is easier for students to work with. If students are willing to take your contracts class to their workout on the treadmill so they can listen to it again, what could possibly be wrong with that? It is also another example of how the use of technology can support the students' autonomy.

Even if a teacher does not digitally capture a class, the students may be doing it anyway. Many laptops today have built-in microphones. It is a simple matter for a student to turn on the microphone at the beginning of class while also taking notes as the class proceeds. The notes are automatically synchronized with the audio file so that when the student is reviewing the notes later, he or she can hear that portion of the class again to make sure it was captured correctly, or just simply for review. Again, what could possibly be wrong with that? It is another way for students to reduce the amount of transcribing they may be doing in class, and it creates a much more useful tool for review than simple notes do.

One of the critical problems for lawyers of the future is the large data set. An example of this would be the explosive growth of electronic discovery described in Chapter 4. If an attorney cannot effectively manage a massive database of e-mails produced in discovery by the opposing party, his representation of the client will be compromised. With large data sets, boolean logic search strings can only get you so far. Fortunately, there are a number of technologies that are developing to graphically map large data sets so they can be used and interpreted. Devon Agent, which will search a large data set and produce a visual diagram of the relationships in that data set, is the sort of tool that students well need to be taught how to use. There will be other emerging technologies to address this critical concern over the next few years.

Other important maturing technologies are the increasingly reliable and effective methods for providing distance learning via the Internet. We have had correspondence courses for many decades and television-based distance learning for nearly that long, but those two distance learning methods have relied on the mail or broadcast television. With the growth of the Internet, it was natural for distance learning to migrate to that platform. For some time the growth of distance learning on the Internet was hampered by a lack of sufficient bandwidth. And while bandwidth was still limited, the software to deliver distance learning over the Internet was still in its early stages and generally in the "not working yet" stage. However, with the rapid expansion of cable-based high-bandwidth forms of Internet access the first problem has largely been solved. The "bugs" have mostly been fixed as well. It is now possible to teach classes, even teach entire courses, over the Internet. The teacher can be there on the screen to lead the class and everyone can hear each other and view a PowerPoint or a whiteboard together. The difference between a conducted live online or live in a physical classroom has narrowed to near insignificance. It is even possible to include video in these classes, and again, there is now generally sufficient bandwidth to support even video applications online.

Yet another example of a maturing technology that can be applied to law school is computer-based MindMapping. While we have always been able to draw diagrams — on paper, with chalk or on whiteboards, computer-based Mind-Mapping supports diagramming of complex legal topics in ways that make it easier and more flexible than the old methods. With programs such as MindManager, Omnigraffle and Inspiration, students can create diagrams on the fly, and adjust them and refine them easily. They can also expand and contract portions of the diagram, an ability that has many uses, including studying for an exam.[106] Many attorneys now use such diagrams to prepare for presentations in court, and some even take them up to the podium when they present their arguments. Here is an example of a student-created mindmap in Administrative law:

---

[106] MICHAEL HUNTER SCHWARTZ, EXPERT LEARNING FOR LAW STUDENTS 164 (2008).

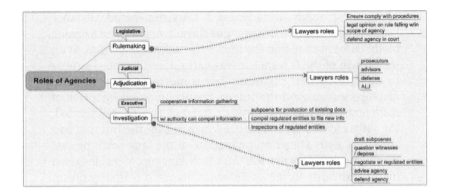

The Educational Technology Maturing Soon

Although many significant technologies have matured over the last few years, there are still others that remain in the "do not work yet" category. Among these is the electronic textbook. All college and graduate students have for many years paid large sums to purchase heavy, cumbersome textbooks for their classes. With the growth of digital technology, many have commented that it would be much better if these books were simply digitized and available to be read on the students' laptops or other devices.

While we are still largely a culture that is used to reading on paper, this may gradually change with the maturing of the Millennial Generation, and there may be some signs that this is happening already. When the University of Phoenix switched to assigning almost entirely digital books, less than 1 percent of students acquired a paper version of the book.[107] Many books used in medical and dental schools are in primarily digital form now. However, a recent study found that 67.3 percent of college students purchasing a textbook preferred paper over a digital book. That percentage increased to 80.1 percent when students were asked their preference for leisure reading. So the electronic textbook seems to be stuck at a transition point between "not working yet" and wide adoption.

---

[107] Mark R. Nelson, E Books in Higher Education, Educause Review, Mar./Apr. 2008, at 51.

At least one legal publishing house has sought to create what it calls an "interactive" casebook series. So far these books have been digital replicas of the printed texts, with hyperlinks to rules and cases added. The problem with this approach is that it is not really interactive, despite the name, and it uses only Web 1.0 technology, thus missing entirely the opportunity to go beyond the limitations of a linear textbook.

Several law professors and commentators have suggested that casebooks should follow the "open source" model. In open source software development, the software "code" is widely available, and improved by many people working cooperatively with one another. Applying the model to casebooks, several professors could write portions of a casebook, and other professors could write other portions. Professors seeking to select a casebook for their courses could then visit a website where they would "assemble" the casebook that they wanted to use from available portions. In this model, once the various portions of a Property casebook (for example) had been created and posted, it would work much like putting together a playlist in iTunes. The output would be a digital PDF file, which could be transmitted to students for printing or reading online.

There are a number of problems with this model as applied to casebooks. First, there is little "scholarly" incentive for a professor to do the work required to post a portion of a casebook that would be valuable to others. They might do it for other purposes, but much of the writing and scholarship created by professors is accomplished within a long-established structure that values and rewards printed scholarship. Second, there are significant copyright concerns. Currently, print publishers play a role in managing copyright licensing as it might apply to portions of the casebooks they publish. An outside entity would have to take on this role, and this would necessitate a pricing structure for each portion of the casebook, since the outside entity is unlikely to do this work for free. As soon as a pricing structure is in place, an entity would have to set that up and that entity would have to take a share. Alas, the desire to get away from the traditional publishing houses still probably leads back to them. But the worst problem with this model is the form of the output. A PDF file is easy to copy and distribute. One student could pay for it and share the cost with fellow students. There are digital rights management (DRM) tools that could be applied to control this, but those are rarely foolproof, and using DRM on these casebooks also runs counter to the whole idea and spirit of the open source movement. Further, portions of the casebook would have to be printed by the student, thus obviating one of the purported benefits. Finally, the output of the open source casebook is still fundamentally in the model of a printed casebook, and would still be taking little or no advantage of the benefits that an online platform could offer to make the entire product more effective and successful as a teaching tool.

What is needed is a hybrid between print and online. Print does certain things well, and online technology does other things well, so we should be creating books that leverage both of those strengths. In all textbooks — certainly this is true of legal textbooks — there are elements that the student really needs to have in print form. An example would be the material that benefits from being highlighted or underlined or book briefed or all three. It is, typically, material that needs to be absorbed slowly. But there is also material — and arguably ought to be more — that involves charts or diagrams which could benefit from being online, and which could provide the student with the ability to interact with what they are learning. Those components should be online, which can support a platform for such display and interactivity.

The best textbooks of the future will look very different from those we have now. Web 2.0 technology can now support some very advanced capabilities, such as animation and clickable and "roll over" interaction. There are many legal concepts that would benefit from animation and interactivity. For example, when a torts professor teaches the *Palsgraf* case, one of the key questions is how the facts explain where the explosion was with respect to the train platform. In a hybrid text model the case would still be printed, but there could also be a reference to the online text where an interactive animation of the explosion could be provided. This way, text does what it does best, and online technologies can supplement and illuminate the text, using capabilities that print cannot offer.

Beyond diagrams and animations, the online portion of a textbook could also add rich media case files, with movies, links to websites and document files. While some books have in the past included a CD-ROM for such materials, having it on a website would be much improved since it can be more interactive and easily updated. Quizzes are already available online in many forms, but the self-assessment and the teaching aspects are not always done so well. The best quizzes for the online portion of a textbook would be ones created by the author, and thus would be tied into the material in the print text. Much of multiple choice testing is primarily about assessment, not about teaching, but ideally all forms of assessment should also have a teaching component. Fortunately, the online platform can help here too. Quizzes in the online portion of a hybrid text could have a branching capability so that, for example, if a student entered a wrong answer to question five, it would branch them to two more "review" questions on the point before allowing the student to go on to question six. This is very hard to do effectively in print, but is easy to do online. Of course, with the quiz being online, it also has the benefit of being self-assessing since student results can automatically be e-mailed to them and entered into a grade book. This is another example of technology supporting ways in which we can address one of the criticisms of legal education by providing the law student with more feedback than students typically receive in law school.

Also integrated into the online portion of the text could be rich case files that would illustrate and illuminate example situations that a lawyer might face in practice. These case files could include PDFs of documents, videos of client interviews, web site links and other supporting materials. The goal here would be to provide information to the students in a practice context, and in forms that a lawyer is likely to see in practice in the future.

Once the online platform for the textbook is in place, it would be a minor matter to include a blog, or a wiki or both. A blog could be used to support journaling, which some teachers ask their students to do as they reflect on what they are learning. And a wiki could be used to support group learning and research projects. An e-mail component should also be included, allowing students to communicate with each other, and making it easy to send quiz results and blog and wiki updates to the professor or teaching assistant.

Another feature of the hybrid textbooks of the future should be to extend the nature and purpose of the teacher's manual. Today, teacher's manuals (TMs) are typically print documents. Being in print form, they are frozen in time, to the period when the textbook was written. Printed teacher's manuals are frozen in another sense, reflecting how the authors believed — at the time they wrote it — their text might or should be used. It would be far better if all teachers' manuals were provided online in the form of a wiki. That way, professors who adopt the text — or who think of doing so — would have access to the wiki TM. Because the TM would be in that form, the professors and the authors could together edit and adjust the TM as time goes on. In this way the adopters could suggest to the authors methods of using the textbook that the authors might not have thought of. Further, in this form the TM becomes — over time — far more useful to new professors considering adoption of the text.

A hybrid textbook would still involve a physical, printed book that is purchased at the campus bookstore as texts always have been. As noted, the printed book would include those materials that students really need in print. But this printed book is smaller and lighter, and it has a code bound into it that the student can use to access the online portion of the book. The combination of the two is what changes the game. Indeed, it could be said that a true hybrid textbook is really not a book anymore — it becomes a new thing we have not yet seen.

Another form of emerging technology that is related to the hybrid textbook is the use of "web widgets" to create interactive web pages that support co-creation of class-related information by students. These information widgets can together create a portal where students can do some "ripping and mixing" what they are learning in the course, that is — they can collect and repurpose web content that relates to the content of the course. Indeed, the online portion of the hybrid textbook could be enabled and enlivened by the use of these technologies as well.

The Adoption of Technology

While the march of technology is inexorable, as has been noted, it also stirs up resistance. Usually the acceptance over time of computer technology goes through at least three phases: early adoption, convenience enthusiasm and finally grudging use by the critical mass. Many believe that the adoption of technology is driven by a coefficient of time and cost. That is, the more time it takes to learn how to use the technology, and the more expensive it is, the lower the adoption rate.

But while time and cost certainly play a role, the greatest resistance to the adoption of technology comes from fear. The people who find themselves at the late adoption end of the spectrum often use the excuses of time and cost. In most cases, though, they are simply fearful that they will not be able to manage the changes the technology requires — or perhaps, that they will break it. It is only when the critical mass grows and the ease of use increases that the late adopters get over their fear.

The early adopters usually have less fear of technology, and the changes it brings. They are typically the sorts of learners who roll up their sleeves and teach themselves how to use the new technology on their own. They have confidence they can apply what they remember how to do from the previous technology they adopted and apply it to the new one. And because they believe that new technology really can improve on what came before, they are willing to invest the energy, time and money required to be an early adopter.

The bridge between the early adopters and the fearful ones are those for whom the technology in question engenders a degree of what could be called convenience enthusiasm. These are people who accept the technology into their lives when they become excited about the convenience that it might bring them. Indeed they have to be enthusiastic, because usually the technology does not "work" at first — at least not as well or reliably as it will later on. A good example of this is found in the adoption of cellular telephones. At first the cost was high, but the early adopters embraced the phones because they loved the mobility and even excitement the gadgets offered. As the phones became more reliable and the cost came down, those who had some degree of enthusiasm for the convenience they offered adopted them. Finally, the last group, the doubters, found the benefits so high that they overcame their grudging fear and bought the phones. Most of us now have cell phones because they are indeed incredibly convenient, helping us keep in touch no matter where we are. Most of us have accepted computers, the Internet, and e-mail into our lives for similar reasons — they make us more efficient in finding information and communicating rapidly with many more people than we could otherwise. Now all these things are so ubiquitous we have stopped noticing them.

It can be expected that the broad adoption in legal education of the sorts of educational technology described in this book will follow a similar path. The early adopters are already in place, and growing. The next step is the critical one: the growth of enthusiasm for the convenience the technology will bring. But before that critical step can take place the connection has to be made between the changes that need to happen in legal education and the role that technology can play in facilitating those changes. Unless we investigate and understand this role, we will never reach a level of broad convenience enthusiasm for leveraging technology in legal education, and finally a level of broad (if grudging) acceptance where truly significant change will finally take place. To fully understand what the careful, broad, and deep application of educational technology can do for legal education we have to investigate its promise in more detail.

Further Reading

MARK WARSCHAUER, LAPTOPS AND LITERACY: LEARNING IN THE WIRELESS CLASSROOM, (2006).

JOHN D. BRANSFORD ET AL., HOW PEOPLE LEARN: BRAIN, MIND, EXPERIENCE, AND SCHOOL (2000).

Susan Swaim Daicoff, LAWYER KNOW THYSELF: A PSYCHOLOGICAL ANALYSIS OF PERSONALITY STRENGTHS AND WEAKNESSES (2004).

HENRY JENKINS ET AL., MACARTHUR FOUND., CONFRONTING THE CHALLENGES OF PARTICIPATORY CULTURE: MEDIA EDUCATION FOR THE 21ST CENTURY (2006).

Chapter 7

THE PROMISE OF TECHNOLOGY

Technology has offered promises before and often failed to deliver on them. At a minimum, solutions to problems facilitated by technology usually take much longer to support real change than all the early predictions that were offered. Developing technological solutions to problems is almost always harder to accomplish, costs more, and takes longer than we think it will. This can be frustrating, and often leads to skepticism.

Over the last decade or so many law schools have formed "technology committees" to examine and experiment with applications of technology in the classroom. These have lead to screens being installed in most law school classrooms, the furnishing of laptops to professors, and high-tech podiums that connect the two. These developments have mostly lead to the proliferation of the use of PowerPoint — with generally dubious results overall. We have again been lead to disappointment, having discovered that "death by PowerPoint" is often just another way to bore our students. The promise of technology seems again to have fallen short. This is especially unfortunate because many teachers have been disillusioned by such early and over-hyped efforts. So we have disengaged, or found ourselves stuck in the PowerPoint rut.

The main premise of this book is that technology is finally entering an era when it will begin to live up to its promises and facilitate real change for the better in legal education. We now have software tools that can help us achieve pedagogical goals we could never achieve before. We have web-based tools such as wikis that can provide a new kind of platform for group work, both for learning and assessment. For those teachers who have wished to engage their students in reflective learning exercises, or to bring practitioners into the discussion, blogs can provide the perfect platform for these forms of learning. And we finally have technologies that can directly facilitate engagement in class such as the thoughtful use of clickers. Perhaps most importantly, online tools for instruction and assessment are finally maturing to the point where they can extend the reach of the faculty, and leverage our most scarce and expensive resources.

What follows in this chapter are examples of the use of some of these emerging technologies by the author over the last four years. These efforts came out of the belief that these tools were finally beginning to mature to the point where substantive pedagogical goals could be achieved in a way we could only dream of just a few years ago. In myriad ways, the pedagogical goals described here and facilitated with technology are consonant with the recommendations for change in legal education described in Chapter 5. Among these are: increasing student engagement, broadening opportunities for skills training, increasing feedback, and involving students in collaborative, experiential forms of learning in courses that are designed to teach theory in the context of practice. They do not, of course, achieve all of these goals perfectly; there is much work left to be done. But these examples are offered here as a starting point, and as support for the premise of this book: that technology can finally help facilitate and lubricate some of the changes that are being proposed for legal education.

The Student Response System

The standard lecture class format, familiar to everyone who has been to college, will always serve an important purpose in education, and law school is no exception. There simply are subjects — or more likely portions of subjects —

that will always need this sort of treatment. One of the reasons this is true, of course, is that non-lecture teaching activities (such as group exercises) are hard to do without some foundational material being provided where everyone in the class is together at the same time. The problems in legal education arise when the lecture format is overused and opportunities for more interactive modes of instruction are overlooked, or worse, never attempted. This is when students disengage, and when their learning suffers. Student response systems, known as clickers, can help by increasing student engagement, especially in a large class environment.

Placing a short clicker quiz in a law school class can have many pedagogical benefits, depending on when it is placed in the class, and the objective of the quiz. At the beginning of a class, it could serve the purpose of solidifying and reviewing concepts from the reading or the previous class. In the middle of class, a quiz could be designed to be a check-in with students to test the level of comprehension of subjects just covered in the lecture. At the end of class, it could be designed to inform the teacher about which concepts might need to be reviewed at the beginning of the next class. These short comprehension quizzes can have grade consequences or not, but either way the engagement level is likely to increase. If students know that they are about to be quizzed on subjects being discussed, they are likely to be more engaged whether the quiz has direct grade consequences or not. And since students want to know how they are doing when they are learning new material the immediate feedback afforded by these clicker quizzes can be powerful. It also partially addresses one of the strongest recommendations of the 2007 Carnegie report, which noted, as we have seen, that many law students graduate without having received sufficient feedback.[108] Also, as noted in Chapter 3, the present generation of students is used to nearly instant responses and results from various forms of digital media. But there is also something about this technology that students find engaging on its own. Being able to click and see the clicker number change color seems to have its own value. It is a physical object that actually involves the student in a physical activity

---

[108] CARNEGIE 2007, *supra* note 14, at 164–67.

in class that also helps kinesthetic and tactile learners. And it is certainly an interface — the remote control — that our students are intimately familiar with.

But the most interesting uses of clickers in the law school classroom are non-quiz uses. Indeed, a more nuanced use of this technology to increase class discussion can be even more engaging for students. In my administrative law class, instead of a quiz with some grade consequence, I would often put up a question solely for the purpose of enhancing the discussion. Usually, this would be the kind of classic law school question that engenders no response — with students suddenly finding an interest in their shoelaces. (We have all experienced this sort of awkward moment in our classes). An example might be: "Is it good public policy for agencies to engage in a cost/ benefit analysis as part of all rulemaking proceedings?" Often, the dead silence greeting this sort of question has come from the students' fear of responding and being the only one in the room to answer in a particular way. Or the assurance level of the students' knowledge — which is, of course, being constructed on the fly during the class — may not yet have reached a point where they are comfortable with the answer and do not want to be publicly exposed as having a less than fully formed answer at the ready. With the clickers, however, all my students could respond electronically (and to each other, anonymously) and I could then show a graph of the responses by category. Once the students realized they were not the only ones with a particular viewpoint, they eagerly raised their hands to answer when I asked for a volunteer.

Another use of clickers might be to ease matters when a teacher poses a question to which the answer might be sensitive. An example of this use might be: "How many students in this class have experienced discrimination in the workplace?" When using their clickers to answer, the students can switch them around, exchanging them randomly with other students sitting near them. This way they know the answer to the sensitive question cannot be traced to them individually. If the resulting graph indicates significant numbers in the class have had this sort of experience, it serves to underscore the importance of the case under discussion — in this instance, of course, involving discrimination law.

Other times in my own teaching I have displayed a question designed to "take the temperature" of the class to see if it was safe to move on to the next topic. Sometimes the answer has been strongly in the right direction, sometimes not. I have then adjusted the rest of the class based on its "temperature" at that particular point. This technology allows the class to tell the teacher when he or she is going too fast. It also gives the students some control over the pace of the proceedings, which, among other benefits, provides them with a measure of autonomy support.

The Use of Wikis in Administrative Law

Administrative law is one of the courses students love to hate. This is particularly true in schools where it is a required course, since many students in the class would not take it otherwise, and so gripe about the requirement. The problem with Admin law — for both the teacher and the student — is that it is such a vast topic that teaching it in a manner students can comprehend is more difficult than usual.

For teachers, what is interesting about a wiki is that it is designed to support collaborative writing — for which opportunities abound in most law school courses. If you are a supporter of the benefits of collaborative learning in law school — even generally so — you might be interested in integrating a wiki site into your teaching. But in Admin law, there are at least two good and enlivening ways to use a wiki. First, the teacher can set up a wiki so the students can write the outline for the course collaboratively. Second, the teacher can set up small group wikis for research projects on particular agencies.

Of course, like everything else, the devil is in the details. The wiki course outline might be a tough sell. Many law teachers have been concerned about the influence that the varied availability of outlines might have on student grades. Some students get good outlines and others do not, and it seems obvious that this might have an affect on the grade they ultimately receive for the course. If you use the Wiki to have the students in this course prepare the outline together, and then, of course, give them access to the same product (the collaborative outline) for the final exam, that might work well.

What I found when I did this was that several students welcomed the approach, a few resisted it vehemently and the rest were willing to go along with the experiment. A few students dropped the course when I announced that this would be how it would work. The students resisting the idea, it appeared, were mostly the sort who felt they had their own process of getting "A's" figured out and they did not want anyone else to either share it or interfere with it. Those who welcomed it were students of the kind who struggle to prepare outlines or receive outlines for courses and often have to turn to commercial outlines. The commercial ones are always problematic, but can be particularly so for Admin law since it is such a vast topic, and professors teach it in substantially different ways.

In my class, participation in the preparation of the outline amounted to 10 percent of each student's grade and nearly all of them participated. A week before the final exam, at the final review class, the students were each provided with a printed copy of their collective work product. They were allowed to take this outline and the textbook (only) into the final exam. The final product was an excellent outline for the course. It even included several tables and charts — some of which had been supplied as handouts during the course, and others that were prepared from scratch by students.

Another use of wikis in law school courses can be for group projects. One of the problems of teaching Admin law is that it often seems disconnected from the agencies that are involved in the cases. You can teach the principle from the case, but simultaneously teaching students how the relevant agency operates can be difficult. In addition, one of the critical skills for attorneys who practice administrative law is the ability to navigate and evaluate the operative aspects of the bureaucracy in which their client is entangled. As a result, in administrative practice, research skills are especially important.

In my Admin law class, the students divided into small groups to study one or another of 10 different federal agencies. These were agencies that were involved in some of the seminal Admin law cases, and ones that would probably be interesting to the students such as the EPA, the

FCC, and OSHA. Each group used a wiki to prepare a site with information about its assigned agency. During the last 20 minutes of the second class each week, a group presented its wiki to the class. All the wikis were available for other students to access, but the small group members were the only ones who could build the site for their assigned agency. The wikis and the matching presentations amounted to 20 percent of their grade for the course.

The students really seemed to enjoy this process. Most of the groups went above and beyond and created extraordinary sites about their agencies adorned with pictures, cartoons and logos. The sites often included numerous links to sources outside the wiki, drawn from within the agency itself, and from sources that criticized or commented on the operation of the agency. At the end of the course the students were given a CD-ROM of all the presentations, which contained a total 88 megabytes of information. Here is a screen shot of the opening page for the wiki site these students prepared:

Administrative Law - Professor Thomson

Group Projects - Fall 2006

Agriculture - U.S. Forest Service (USFS)

Lindsay McKay, Hunter Puckett, Christine Thornton, Jonathan Shultz

Transportation - Federal Aviation Administration (FAA)

Amy Goscha, Steven Blarr, Ricki Kelly, Brian Eckhardt

Labor - Occupational Safety and Health Administration (OSHA)

Mike Benschneider, Beth Tomerlin, Erin O'Leary, Luke Sherman

Commerce - National Oceanic and Atmospheric Administration (NOAA)

Helaine Powell, Laura Guice

This is an example of the use of wikis in one law course. But the possibilities for the use of this technology in many law school courses are vast. In any law class where the professor asks students to work on problems in small groups, and for which the output is something written, a wiki is a great fit. One of the best things about wikis, of course, is that they are online and asynchronous. Our students move around and are used to being both mobile and connected, so they appreciate the flexibility and convenience afforded by doing part of their coursework online in a group setting. It is hard for students to all meet in one study room at one particular time outside of class (and this is acutely true for evening students). These logistical problems can actually interfere with collaborative learning methods for law students. If a course's objective (or part of it) is for students to work collaboratively in small groups — and there are many good reasons to have such an objective — wikis are an ideal solution.

The Use of File and Serve in a Litigation Course

Applications of technology to teaching can also be effective in increasing student engagement even if the educational objectives involved are relatively small. I teach a practice-focused course called Discovery Practicum that focuses on the process of civil discovery. During the term, students represent either the plaintiff or the defendant in a rather simple contract dispute between two companies. At the beginning, the students are given a small portion of their client's file. As they learn about each form of discovery, they prepare the appropriate discovery document and serve it on their assigned opposing counsel. In the first such assignment, the students prepare a set of interrogatories and serve their opposing counsel at the next class. They also receive a set of interrogatories. That class is about answering interrogatories, and the next assignment is for them to prepare answers to the interrogatories that they received. This pattern repeats through the course through document requests (and answers), requests for admission (and answers), and the preparation for depositions. In the deposition phase, the student each take, defend, and act as a witness in three different depositions transcribed by a student court reporter.

Although I first taught this course in 1993, it achieves one of the primary recommendations of the 2007 Carnegie Report — to teach rules and cases in context. Part of the class time has to be in lecture since the course must cover the applicable rules and the governing case law. But the main thrust of the course is practical, consisting of the to-and-fro of a mock litigation.

To make it even more realistic, I also enlisted the relevant technology. As noted in Chapter 4, a growing feature of law practice is electronic filing in court, with a concomitant electronic serving of the same document on opposing counsel. Accordingly, I approached the people at File & Serve, a service widely used across the country, including Colorado, where I teach. They agreed to set up a "mock court" on their File & Serve system for my students to use for filing and serving all of their documents in the case. Every assignment is filed in the mock case for each pair of counsel for plaintiff and defendant. When the filing is complete, the opposing attorney receives an e-mail notifying him or her, and can go to the File & Serve system and download the document. The "Judge" — in this case, me — also receives notice of the filing, and there is a different interface where the Judge can review all the filings in each of the cases.

To sum up, while rules and case law are covered in depth, the design of the course is intended for students to learn the law of discovery in context, and to also prepare them for the sort of work they will encounter in practice.

The Use of CaseMap in Teaching LRW

CaseMap is a database program used in hundreds of law offices across the country to track the details of individual cases. The best way to think about what CaseMap does is to think of it as a series of spreadsheets with deep linking between them. If you think of a spreadsheet that lists details about the facts of a case, and another that lists the details of documents that relate to the case (and that can link to electronic copies of each document), then you have a good idea of how attorneys might use it in practice. Then, add a spreadsheet with details about the legal research that might pertain to the problem, and then add one more: an outline of key issues in the case. So far, that is four of these spreadsheets. The next step is to create links between them that illustrate associations between your legal research and certain legal issues, or between certain facts and the documents from which they came, or the issues that they support, or all of these.

There are only a few more details that are important. First, there are several more spreadsheets that I did not describe. Second, the program is highly customizable, so you can easily change the column headings to redesign the default spreadsheets to organize the information as a particular case requires. Third, the spreadsheets have sophisticated sorting capabilities, so it is easy to display only certain data in the spreadsheet, to design a printout on just one issue, or to display only relevant case law (as opposed to statutory law, or secondary sources), for example.

Most important, this software is in wide use in law firms and government offices around the country. If this were a technology that no lawyer ever used to organize details of a case it would give me pause to use it for that purpose in class. It would still be useful, but somehow it is good to know that all the United States Attorneys' offices have licensed it, and the War Crimes Tribunals at The Hague use it to manage their cases.

In the legal writing course, professors usually assign several writing projects each semester, meet with students to answer questions, and then students submit their written product. The teacher then comments extensively on the written assignment and returns it to the student.[109] Sometimes this is followed with another conference, sometimes not. A few teachers will ask for and comment heavily on draft documents, but this is relatively rare.[110] As a result of this process, it is unfortunate that legal writing teachers are often in the same position as doctors who are asked for a diagnosis after the body is already dead: the papers have been written, and the mistakes have been made. The legal writing teacher must then deduce where the student went wrong. The problem is that there are typically two kinds of writing

---

[109] AM. BAR ASS'N, SOURCEBOOK ON LEGAL WRITING PROGRAMS 41–44 (2006), [hereinafter "SOURCEBOOK".]

[110] SOURCEBOOK, *supra* note 109 at 45, n. 24.

problems on the students' papers we see: those that are pure writing problems, and those that are writing problems *that were caused by thinking problems.* Unfortunately, it is often hard to separate the two, since they are often intertwined.

An integral component of nearly all legal writing courses is some form of training in legal research, typically both in the book form and the online form.[111] Most programs use some form of research exercise in the library to supplement their teaching of how the physical books are used and interrelate. Most programs also offer training on how to use the major online legal research services, LexisNexis and Westlaw.[112]

Typically, in the fall semester, most legal writing courses are focused on teaching the objective form of legal writing used in legal memoranda. Many legal writing teachers (although not all) allow students to conduct their own research — either in the library or online — to support their work on one or more of those memo assignments.[113] During this phase in the fall semester, most teachers assign students to prepare and submit some form of "Research Log," denoting what research path they followed and what they found. This is done primarily for two reasons: 1) so the teacher can assess how well the student learned the basic legal research concepts that were covered in the course, and 2) so the teacher can assess how close the student came to finding the right material. Many teachers would also say that an additional pedagogical purpose of the research log assignment is to teach students the value of keeping track of their research as it progresses. Traditionally, however, the

---

[111] SOURCEBOOK, *supra* note 109 at 20–27.

[112] SOURCEBOOK, *supra* note 109 at 22–23.

[113] In contrast, there are several programs where it is more common to assign the fall memo in a "closed" context, where the key statute and cases are supplied to the students instead of allowing them to find them on their own. This is usually done in the belief that the teacher wants the student to focus on the writing instead of getting lost in the research process. The countervailing view is that if we are teaching legal research in the fall, we might as well let them exercise those skills as they are learning them, with the understanding that they may need more guidance during this period. Among those programs that assign "closed memos" in the fall, all of them assign open memo research problems in the spring semester.

focus of the assignment was to assess the quality of the research process, not how well the student organized the material they found. Here is a diagram that represents this pedagogical goal, in which the work being assessed by the teacher is in the breakout portion on the right. Figure 1:

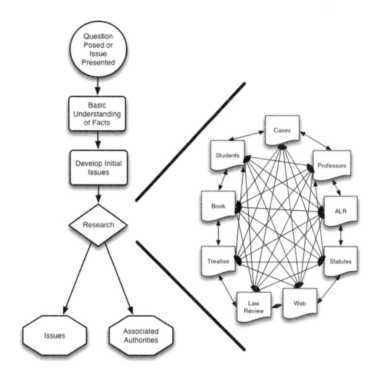

In my own program — prior to the implementation of CaseMap — the research log assignment involved a printed chart that students filled out as they went along in their research.[114] But these research logs did little to require the

---

[114] The four column headings on the Chart were: "Descriptive Words and Key Numbers;" "Citations Found;" "Comments — Was Case Positive, Negative, or Useless?;" and "Research Status — Updated or Shepardized? (Date)."

student to describe or depict their actual thought process as they were conducting the research, and, as a result, it was difficult or impossible to assess how they were doing in that step. That thought process might be fairly depicted by this diagram. Figure 2:

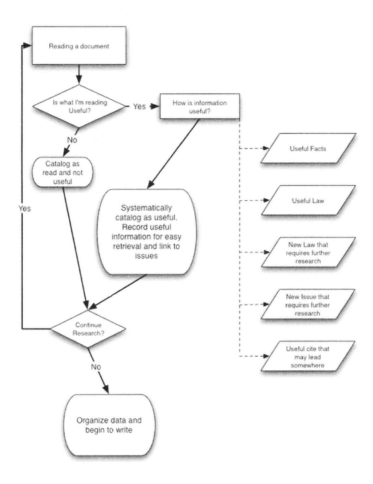

It has long occurred to me that if we could help the student during the critical "thinking and linking" process that we know has to precede good legal writing, the student might then produce a memo at the end of the process that only (or primarily) had pure writing problems.[115] Put another way, if we could diagnose the problem before the "body was dead," we could help our students produce better final products. But practically speaking, this is impossible (or nearly so). In other words, since we can not sit with each student individually while they are making the "thinking and linking" associations as they are doing their research and organizing the information they have into an outline for the memo or brief we have asked them to write.[116]

CaseMap is the first program I have seen that actually allows a teacher to enter into the students' thought process, to "take a trip into their heads," and help them learn how to develop the important pre-writing thinking skills in any systematic way. This is mostly because the teacher can require the student to systematically report on the current state of their research and thinking, and it can thereby illustrate the critical linking and categorization that must be done before the writing begins. While the diagram in Figure 1 above is focused on the quality of the research process, and the diagram in Figure 2 above is an interim filtering step during the research process, the diagram in Figure 3 illustrates the categorizing and "funneling" of the research a student has found into specific issues that need to be addressed in the document they are about to write. Figure 3:

---

[115] Of course, to some extent, we were able to do this before CaseMap. Occasionally a student will say something in a conference, or will come in to ask a question, and we can tell from their question that their thinking is off somehow. But this is fairly haphazard, and not easy to do. Those that use the same memo problem every year may also be better at doing this. *See*, Ellie Margolis & Susan L. DeJarnatt, MOVING BEYOND PRODUCT TO PROCESS: BUILDING A BETTER LRW PROGRAM, 46 SANTA CLARA L. REV. 93, 131–134 (2005).

[116] Instead, we approximate that goal, by discussing the problem in class, or by meeting with students either in scheduled conferences or in office hours.

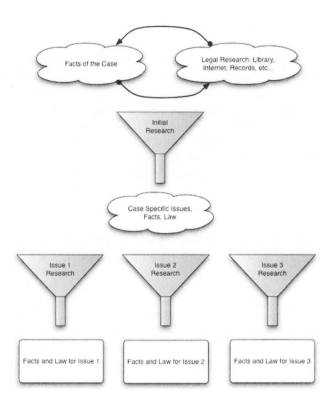

This last step, which usually takes place just prior to the writing, is rarely something that legal writing professors get to see. CaseMap, on the other hand, can be configured[117] to allow the teacher to observe the student's "funneling" process in a systematic way and to help them with it. In addition, simply emphasizing this step, and creating an assignment

---

[117] One of the ways to configure CaseMap for this pedagogical purpose is to create a "shell file" for students to use as they start their research. CaseMap is a large program with many features, so by creating a dummy file with the columns and data entry points students need already set up, CaseMap can be constrained to your specific teaching requirements.

around it, also has the added benefit of encouraging the student to focus on the importance of it.[118]

In my legal writing course, I ask students to complete a specific CaseMap assignment showing this "thinking and linking" process, and immediately after it is due I meet with the students to go over their CaseMap reports. Because the reports are uniform in purpose and design, I can easily compare "apples to apples." As a result, I can quickly tell what sources students have found, but even more importantly, what they are doing with what they have found. I can tell what they have missed, and sometimes I will help them fill that "pothole" in their research, which may otherwise have lead to a writing problem in the final product. And most importantly, I can tell if they are going through an appropriate "funneling" process in identifying the important issues, and marshalling the right research materials to describe each issue (in a memo) or advocate on their client's behalf (in a brief). This aspect of the process is evident in their CaseMap reports in two ways: first, in the text they chose to excerpt from the case law they found and second, in the linking they make between those excerpts and the issues screen (or outline) of the memo they are about to start writing. If they are struggling with those critical steps, I can spend more time in the conference discussing the process with them.

In the fall semester, I give my students two assignments to complete. The first is to fill out the "Facts" and the "Objects" spreadsheets in CaseMap. Students are asked to fill in these sheets with the details of the problem that they have been assigned and print it out for my review. This assignment was primarily conceived as a way to have the students become more familiar with the program before getting into the more substantive use of it.

---

[118] In a new groundbreaking study, Professor Anne Enquist of Seattle University School of Law has found that the most successful students in the legal writing class are the ones who systematically organize their research materials before writing, including the use of a notebook of printed cases. The most successful student in this study commented that "if he had the project to do over, he would have made a chart summarizing the cases, their holdings, and their application to factors." Anne M. Enquist, *Unlocking the Secrets of Highly Successful Legal Writing Students*, 82 St. John's L. Rev. 609 (2008).

The second and more substantive assignment is to have my students fill out the "Extracts from Authorities" spreadsheet and the "Issues" spreadsheet in CaseMap while they were conducting their research and preparing to write the memo. I ask them to create an outline of their memo in the Issues spreadsheet[119] and then link that back to their research and, most particularly, to the most relevant "extract" portions from the case and statutory law that they have found in their research. Once they have completed this work, they are ready for the conference in which I review it with them. Here is what the Extracts from Authorities screen looks like when a student completes the assignment:

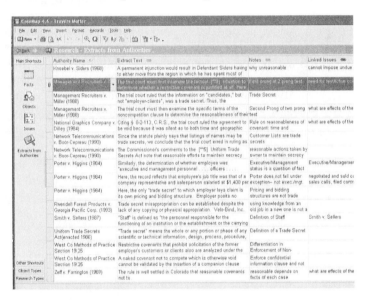

Generally speaking, the students accepted CaseMap and understood its benefits. As a measure of this acceptance, in the first year of the program, only nine students complained about it in over 300 student evaluations, and a few mentioned it favorably. Given that legal writing is often the course that students most complain about, because it is so difficult, that is not an especially poor rate. In the years

---

[119] The Issues spreadsheet in CaseMap is the equivalent of an outliner program.

following, the number of complaints expressed in the student evaluations remained about the same.

As you might expect, some students took to it quickly; some even used it for other classes. Over the last few years, several students have indicated that they got summer jobs in the after their first and second years because the law firm they were applying to used it and was favorably impressed with their ability to use it.

The Use of Online Pedagogy to Teach Law

Online learning, once thought of as impossible or ineffective,[120] is becoming increasingly common.[121] Corporations have widely adopted it,[122] and the academy is starting to accept it as well. There are numerous college-level courses,[123] and even a few law school classes,[124] that are taught fully online. One law professor and former Dean has recently suggested that teaching more courses online might be one way to reign in the soaring costs of a legal education.[125]

In the fall of 2002, slightly more than 1.6 million students took at least one online course at a U.S. degree granting institution. In the fall of 2006, that number was 3.2 million.[126] The recent report from the Department of

---

[120] Debby Goldberg, *Learning from a Distance*, WASH. POST, April 5, 1998, at R4.

[121] I. Elaine Allen & Jeff Seaman, *Making the Grade: Online Education in the United States, 2006* (2006).

[122] Paul Rew, *Education and Services: Web of Compliance*, LEGAL TIMES, June 16, 2006.

[123] Peter Appelbome, *Distance Learning: Education.com*, N.Y. TIMES, April 4, 1999, at A26. In the spring semester of 2006, the University of Massachusetts had 9,200 students taking courses online, Penn State had 5, 691, and the University of Maryland had 51,450 in its University College program. Daniel Golden, *Degrees@StateU.edu, Online University Enrollment Soars as Quality Improves*, WALL ST. J., May 9, 2006, at B1.

[124] Robert M. Lloyd, INVESTIGATING A NEW WAY TO TEACH LAW: A COMPUTER BASED COMMERCIAL LAW COURSE, 50 J. LEGAL EDUC. 587 (2000). *See also* footnotes 18–21, *supra*.

[125] Daniel J. Morrissey, SAVING LEGAL EDUCATION, 56 J. LEGAL EDUC. 254, 278 (2006).

[126] *Allen and Seaman, supra* note 3, at 5.

Education about the increase of technology in learning noted this about the growth of online learning: "over the past five years there has been explosive growth in online and multimedia instruction (e-learning) and 'virtual schools.' At least 15 states now provide some form of virtual schooling to supplement regular classes or provide for special needs. Hundreds of thousands of students are taking advantage of e-learning this school year. About 25 percent of all K-12 public schools now offer some form of e-learning or virtual school instruction. Within the next decade every state and most schools will be doing so."[127]

To date, in law schools, the number of students taking an online course has been significantly smaller because so far only a few law schools offer online classes. This is partly because the ABA (which accredits law schools) limits the number of credits a law student may take in their course of study to 12 and only four per term.[128] In addition, only students with 28 credits already completed toward their degree may enroll in an online course.[129]

The ABA standards define a distance learning course as one that entails "an educational process characterized by the separation, in time or place, between instructor and student."[130] It allows a law school to award credit for a distance course so long as: there is "ample interaction" between the instructor and the students,[131] and there is "ample monitoring" of student effort and achievement through the progression of the course.[132] Neither of these two requirements is described or defined in greater detail.

Despite these limiting factors, several law schools have developed and offer doctrinal courses online. Professor Peter Martin at Cornell Law School has taught a course in Social

---

[127] Technology Plan, *supra* note 18, at 34.

[128] American Bar Association, Section of Legal Education & Admissions to the Bar, Law School Accreditation Standard 306(b) [hereinafter Accreditation Standard].

[129] Accreditation Standard 306(d).

[130] Accreditation Standard 306(b).

[131] Accreditation Standard 306(c)(1).

[132] Accreditation Standard 306(c)(2).

Security Law for the last six years that attracts many students from other law schools.[133] Adjunct Professor Don Smith of the Sturm College of Law at the University of Denver has taught a course in European Union Law for the last four years, attracting students from other law schools as well. Pace Law School briefly offered a course in Health Care Fraud and Abuse Law to both students and practitioners.[134] And Professor Michael Perlin at New York Law School offers an online course in Mental Disability Law that even attracts students from overseas.[135] So far, these online substantive law courses seem to have three things in common: they are in a relatively narrow field that may not have a high student subscription in their own school, they offer subjects that might well be of interest to students at other schools, and they have in fact been offered to students outside of their sponsoring school. If the trend of offering courses to students outside the particular law school that sponsors them continues and broadens, it could have interesting implications for the current structure of the legal academy, since many students might routinely take up to 12 credits at other institutions, thus creating a tuition deficit at their own institution. Such a potential deficit might cause that institution to develop its own courses. So far, however, no such trend has developed.[136]

When I was first asked to teach a legal research and writing (LRW) course online, I was concerned about my ability to translate the requirements of the course to a fully online environment. With students spread around the country — some of whom I would never physically meet in person — it seemed a daunting challenge to achieve the generally accepted educational goals of the course. I quickly

---

[133] *See*, Peter W. Martin, Information Technology and U.S. Legal Education: Opportunities, Challenges, and Threats 52 J. of Legal Educ. 506 (2002).

[134] Linda C. Fentiman, A Distance Education Primer: Lessons from My Life as a Dot.Edu Entrepreneur, 6 N.C. J. L. & Tech. 41, 62 (2004).

[135] http://www.nyls.edu/pages/389.asp (last visited May 9, 2008).

[136] It should be noted, however, that Concord Law School, owned by Kaplan, Inc., offers a fully online program of study in the law. This program, however, is not accredited by the American Bar Association, for the reasons described *supra* at notes 14–17.

discovered that over the last decade there has been considerable debate about whether "physical proximity" is a necessary component of the learning process.[137] I also learned that other possible pitfalls of online education that have been identified in the research are "learner isolation,"[138] and "learner frustration, anxiety, and confusion."[139] Further, it became clear to me that online students need greater discipline and the ability to self motivate than is typically required of students in a ground class.[140] Some students just have a greater need for classroom interaction with their peers than others, and some feel a loss of connection with the teacher in an online class as well.[141]

Armed with an understanding of these concerns about online education, I set out to construct a version of the LRW course for the online environment that would still successfully achieve the generally accepted goals for the course.

---

[137] *See, e.g.,* John J. Ketterer and George E. March II, RE-CONCEPTUALIZING INTIMACY AND DISTANCE IN INSTRUCTIONAL MODELS, 9 ONLINE J. DISTANCE LEARNING ADMIN. (2006), *available* at: http://www.westga.edu/~distance/ojdla/spring91/ketterer91.htm.

[138] K. M. Brown, THE ROLE OF INTERNAL AND EXTERNAL FACTORS IN THE DISCONTINUATION OF OFF-CAMPUS STUDENTS, 17 DISTANCE EDUCATION 14 (1996).

[139] N. Hara & R. Kling, STUDENTS' DISTRESS WITH A WEB-BASED DISTANCE EDUCATION COURSE: AN ETHNOGRAPHIC STUDY OF PARTICIPANTS' EXPERIENCES, 3 INFO., COMM. & SOC'Y 557, 579 (2000).

[140] R. Golladay, V. Prybutok, & R. Huff, CRITICAL SUCCESS FACTORS FOR THE ONLINE LEARNER, 40 J. COMPUTER INFO. SYS. 69 (2000).

[141] Naseem Stecker, LOGGING ON TO A LAW EDUCATION, MICH. BAR J., Mar. 2003, at 42.

Steps to Teaching a Class Online:

1. Learn the Available Technology

2. Set Educational Goal for Each Class or Module

3. Select the Technology that Best Supports Achieving the Goal

4. Roll Out Technology and Test

5. Evaluate and Adjust as Needed

The first thing is to learn the available technology. Fortunately, there are now a plethora of tools to deliver instructional materials online, and they are increasing in number, sophistication, and reliability. The most important of these tools most LRW teachers already use and are quite familiar with: an online courseware system, such as TWEN or Blackboard. In the "ground" version of the class LRW professors typically use these in a supplemental role (to post PowerPoints from class for example). But in the online class the courseware system becomes the surrogate for the classroom. This makes it even more imperative to learn the various extensions and additional capabilities beyond what you might use in a ground class that the courseware systems offer[142] so that you might leverage them to achieve your goals for the course. In addition, although these systems are becoming more feature rich over time, there are many other technologies that exist outside of those systems that can be employed in support of online education. A careful study of those capabilities is a good first step in the process of developing an online law school course.

The next step is to decide what your educational goal is for each class or module of the course, and then to pick the technology that best supports achieving that goal. This deceptively simple step is actually the most difficult because it requires a re-conceptualization of each component of the

---

[142] In particular, Blackboard is becoming a platform that various schools and developers are writing add in "blocks" to extend the functionality of the courseware system. TWEN, a proprietary system owned by West Publishing, is not so open, and thus not extensible by outside developers.

course that you teach in the classroom and a thoughtful application of the panoply of available technologies to each component.

Unfortunately, many online courses either skip this step or give it insufficient attention. They may post a PowerPoint, and set up a discussion board about it, and call that a "class." Even worse, some courses will follow that same structure for every class, with no effort to select a particular technology to support a particular educational goal. This sort of online course design misses the opportunities afforded by the developing technology of online course delivery, and it may even contribute to the isolation and frustration experienced by many online students.

In the online legal writing course that I teach, I use five different online modalities to deliver the content of the course. They are: seven online PowerPoints with audio voice-over, three online exercises, two asynchronous forum discussions, two individual telephone calls with each student, and four live (i.e., synchronous) classes where every one is online together at the same time. To avoid confusion as to what is required of the student at any given time, I provide a color-coded syllabus, together with a course policies document that describes each of these course modalities in detail. Of course, there is also a textbook for the class, with reading assignments prior to each class, and there are written papers that have to be submitted and which I comment on, grade, and return electronically.[143]

Simply put, in developing the syllabus, I went through a process where I decided what the educational goal of each class would be, and then selected a technology that I felt would support that goal most effectively. So, for example, if at a particular point in the course I want the students to get some basic information that adds to their assigned reading prior to class, I will prepare a PowerPoint, much as many teachers do in any regular class. But in a ground class, the teacher is physically there and is often supplementing the content of the PowerPoint with a lecture that is integrated

---

[143] Note that in this online course, there was no oral argument at the end, as there traditionally is at the end of most legal writing courses. Of course, a very effective substitute could be accomplished via videoconference.

with it. So simply posting it for someone to click through by themselves is far less effective than what we do in the classroom. So I added my voice over the PowerPoint using a free tool from Microsoft called Producer and a microphone. Once the process is complete, the resulting files must be uploaded to a website for access by students. I post them to my faculty website and link that location into the Blackboard site for the course, so to the student it looks as though the PowerPoint is built into Blackboard, when in fact it resides on my website.

At a few points in the semester, I felt like nothing could replace the ability for us to all be in the same "room" at the same time. An example was a class in which we conduct mock settlement negotiations, and I assign groups of students to represent each party in a lawsuit. These "synchronous" classes mimic a real class in many respects, except that we can not see each other. In the past few years, the software I have used to deliver these classes is called Wimba Live Classroom, which I have found to be exceedingly effective.[144] This module requires that everyone in the class have a microphone and headset (or equivalent). Students must also install and configure certain software before they can access the class.[145] While that sounds daunting, in my experience it has worked well, and students have not been concerned about purchasing the headset or frustrated by the software configuration. As a threshold matter, it almost goes without saying that these technologies have to work. There is nothing worse than trying to conduct a class where only half of the students are online and the other half are trying to get online and getting frustrated. It is wise to have a "dry run" of whatever software you choose prior to the scheduled time for the first synchronous class in a semester.

As a substantive pedagogical matter, when I have conducted these "live" classes, I have found them to take the point of difference between an online class and a

---

[144] Information about Wimba Live Classroom and a demo can be found at this location: http://www.wimba.com/products/wimbaclassroom.

[145] The process of installing and configuring the required software is automated by a wizard that automatically launches when the "Live Classroom" is launched for the first time.

"ground" class very near to the vanishing point. Indeed, some of these classes have rivaled some of my best classes in the traditional classroom. I usually post a PowerPoint that everyone can see, and as I work my way through it, I occasionally stop and encourage a discussion on a particular point, much as I would do in a physical classroom. When a student wishes to speak they can click a button marked with a hand — to simulate that they are "raising their hand" — and I call on them. They then click the "talk" button, and speak. Everyone in the class can hear them. Others may also click the hand button, and I call on them, and they comment on a question I may have posed or on what a classmate has just said. Meanwhile, I am sitting in my comfy chair in my study at home, with my laptop on my lap. And, in a recent class, my students were located in Bridgeport, CT, Davenport, IA, Charlestown, SC, and Ignacio, CO, among other locations around the country. Yet the distance between us faded away and we were all "together" at one time, in one "place." Here is a screenshot of a class in the Wimba Live Classroom software:

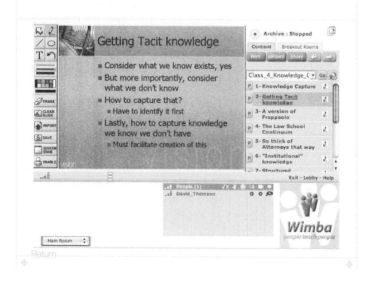

However, not all classes require this intimacy and replacing a traditional class with only a series of "live" classes would be problematic. One of the things that attract students to online classes is the flexibility they afford,[146] and the matter of getting everyone on different time zones to "meet" at a particular time is not a simple one. As a result, I save the "live" classes for those modules of the course that truly require us to all be together at the same time.

Since one of the chief concerns about online education is the physical distance that exists between the teacher and student, I selected these modalities to achieve the educational goal for each class, but also to "bridge the gap" created by the physical distance. The PowerPoints with audio help students to get the additional information that my voice-over contains, but also serves to bridge the gap between me and my students. The synchronous "live" classes also allow more information to be conveyed on the subject, but serve to bridge the gap as well — between me and my students, but also among the students as well.

There are other lower-tech things that can be done to support the same goals. Like many law professors, I have a website,[147] and I refer new students to it prior to the beginning of each class, so they might get to know me better. I ask my students to send me a resume and picture, so I can learn about them and this also gives me a visual image of them as I work with them. I also telephone each of them personally early in the semester to get to know them, and to answer any questions they may have about the course. I encourage them to e-mail me or call me at any time throughout the semester if they have any questions.

Another key component of any legal writing course is the individual conference between teacher and student with a commented written assignment in front of them that they can discuss and review together. To replicate this component of the course, I telephone each student after they have received a version of their written work that I have commented on

---

[146] Henry O'Lawrence, THE INFLUENCES OF DISTANCE LEARNING ON ADULT LEARNERS, 81 TECHNIQUES 47 (2006); Gary Wyatt, SATISFACTION, ACADEMIC RIGOR AND INTERACTION: PERCEPTIONS OF ONLINE INSTRUCTION, 125 EDUC. 460 (2003).

[147] The Author's website may be accessed at this address: http://www.law.du. edu/thomson.

using Word's commenting feature.[148] While there may be dynamics to these "live and in person" conferences that are transmitted via body language[149] — which would be missed while on a telephone call — I have found the telephone conferences to be just as effective as an in person conference. Students seem to ask similar questions in both forms of conference, and on the telephone they can hear my voice explain the concept they are struggling with, which is the most important component of the conference and the reason for having it.

One of the advantages of teaching online is that the distance between the teacher and student can arguably support a *better* environment for learning than a ground class. In his book *Teaching with Your Mouth Shut*, Donald Finkel describes the power and effectiveness of "inquiry-centered teaching."[150] Such teaching is based on the teacher creating an environment — and actively guiding it — where students can make their own inquiry into what they are learning together. In my online classes I have found that I can not "talk" as much, and instead, I have to focus my efforts on creating the best environment for my students' learning. In this way, an online environment almost forces the teacher into the "guide on the side" role and opens up space for students to learn from each other as much as they learn from the teacher.

At first blush, it would seem that successfully teaching legal writing online would be too difficult, if not impossible. After all, in a distance education setting, the foundational aspects of the legal writing course that are provided by face-to-face conferences and live classroom sessions with small class sizes are lost. At a minimum, since these are the foundational aspects of the LRW course with which most of

---

[148] Since we cannot promptly deliver a commented paper to a distance student, it is advisable to comment electronically on their papers, and return them via E-mail.

[149] Robin A. Wellford-Slocum, THE LAW SCHOOL STUDENT-FACULTY CONFERENCE — TOWARD A TRANSFORMATIVE LEARNING EXPERIENCE, 45 S. TEX. L. REV. 255, 302–303 (2004).

[150] DONALD L. FINKEL, TEACHING WITH YOUR MOUTH SHUT, Chapter 4 (2000).

us are familiar, it would be natural to resist a request from a Dean or Director to teach the course online.

But it can be done. It is essential, however, to design the syllabus carefully by leveraging the best technology for the educational goal for each module. And it is also essential — as it is in the classroom environment — to be hyper-organized and clear about what the expectations of the students are at any given time. Commenting on student papers remains important, but returning the papers via e-mail (as opposed to by hand) seems to make no difference. Conferencing can still be very effective if simply conducted over the telephone. Efforts to be accessible and open to your students remain important, as it always has been in the classroom environment.

Understanding the available technology is an essential component of all of this. Increasingly, our students are comfortable with these tools, and they will know when we are not. Fortunately, most law schools have educational technology personnel who can help. But it does require some effort on the part of the teacher.

Conclusion

The promise of technology in legal pedagogy is beginning to be fulfilled, and realistic and useable tools for better and more effective teaching are finally working well. We must learn about, use, and finally embrace these technologies to reach a new generation of student. If we do, we can finally address — in a systematic way — many of the criticisms that have been leveled at legal education for almost 100 years.

Further Reading

Deborah Jones Merritt, *Legal Education in the Age of Cognitive Science and Advanced Classroom Technology* (Ctr. For Interdisciplinary Law & Policy Studies, Working Paper No. 63, 2007), *available at* http://ssrn.com/abstract=1007800.

RENA M. PALLOFF & KEITH PRATT, BUILDING ONLINE LEARNING COMMUNITIES: EFFECTIVE STRATEGIES FOR THE VIRTUAL CLASSROOM (2007).

COMPUTER-SUPPORTED COLLABORATIVE LEARNING: BEST PRACTICES AND PRINCIPLES FOR INSTRUCTORS (Kara L. Orvis & Andrea L. R. Lassiter eds., 2008).

Chapter 8

THE FUTURE FOR LEGAL EDUCATION

In an article published in 2001 entitled "The Happy Charade," two law professors and a researcher at UCLA reported on a survey of law student satisfaction.[151] Their focus was on how to make the third year of law school more effective. As part of their survey, they compared three "Stories" about 3L education that they heard from the survey respondents, which they called the "Official Story," the "Bleak Story" and the "Signal Story." According to the Official Story — usually heard from dean's offices — the third year of law school is required for additional acculturation in the law and to cover additional topics. Third year students are perceived

---

[151] Mitu Gulati et al., THE HAPPY CHARADE: AN EMPIRICAL EXAMINATION OF THE THIRD YEAR OF LAW SCHOOL, 51 J. LEGAL EDUC. 235 (2001).

as very engaged in their studies. In the Bleak Story, the third year of law school is perceived as pointless and students have disengaged; many of them are depressed and feeling alienated from their reasons for going to law school in the first place. In the Signal Story, while it is agreed that the third year is pointless, this is perceived by students as OK[152] since, to them, law school exists primarily to sort and credential the students, and they did not expect anything more. In other words, law schools only exist to serve a "signaling" function to employers of their graduates.

The article concludes that the Signal Story holds up best to the data the authors gathered. In their survey, 48 percent of respondents were "very satisfied with law school, [but] only 12 percent thought school had prepared them very effectively for their careers."[153] The UCLA team cites this as evidence that students only expect law school to serve the sorting and credentialing function. They also note, however, that although generally satisfied, second and third year students are eager to pursue "real interests and develop new, client-oriented skills ... and are seeking opportunities to do pro bono work."[154] The article concludes with some suggestions for making the third year more relevant and useful, but acknowledges that the signaling function serves many interests, and so suggests that changing this construct is not likely.

The conclusion that law schools serve primarily a signaling function may not be wrong, but it is profoundly troublesome. In a world where legal education costs in the neighborhood of $35,000 per year — and many students graduate with more than $100,000 worth of debt[155] — it remains to be seen how long law students will be happy under-utilizing their third year, or where only 12 percent

---

[152] It should be noted that the LSSSE, which is more recent than the survey reported in the article referenced here, supports its conclusions. Law students are generally happy with their law school experience, but they also admit to not getting sufficient feedback, and to not being very engaged in their 3L year.

[153] Gulati, *supra* note 148, at 257.

[154] *Id.* at 259.

[155] LSSSE, *supra* note 86.

think law school has prepared them for practice. Should we not hope for more when we ask students to give us three years of their lives, not to mention their money? We cannot, either ethically or morally, continue to allow the "Happy Charade" to characterize the law school experience. We not only mistreat our students, we do a disservice to the public.

But the Signal Story — and the cynicism contained within it — holds sway because it serves various interests and because the economic model of legal education is based upon it. We all know that we can and should do better, but it is hard to figure out how to get there.

The Clinical Approach in Medical Education

As we saw in Chapter 5, the Carnegie Foundation's Flexner report in 1910 had a profound affect on medical education. It recommended that more clinical rounds be made a significant part of the last two years of medical education, and, over the several years that followed, that actually happened. Over the years since the publication in 1914 of the Redlich report on legal education, many commentators and critics have suggested that legal education should do the same as was done in medical education. Many scholars and lawyers have since recommended that law students should have at least some clinical experience before they graduate. This recommendation was made most recently by Dean Erwin Chemerinsky, who is in the enviable position of creating a law school from the ground up as the recently appointed Dean of the new UC Irvine Law School.[156] And as we saw in Chapter 2, among the many curricular experiments being adopted around the country, Washington and Lee Law School has just simply dispensed with the usual third year of law school and will replace it with an entirely clinical year.

Nobody doubts that there are benefits to a clinical experience in law school. There is simply nothing that replaces interviewing a real client with a real legal problem that a student is able to resolve (or at least go some distance towards resolving). The large experiential benefits from this

---

[156] Chemerinsky, *supra* note 15, at 595.

sort of learning are unquestioned, and it is a style of teaching that fits perfectly with the active learning goals we have discussed, and the preferences and needs of the Millennial Generation explained in Chapter 3. Furthermore, many law school graduates are about to join corporate law firms and therefore will work primarily in a fairly rarified world, perhaps for the rest of their lives. The benefit of having the experience of representing a client before the Social Security Administration in a disability hearing, for example, could be enormous. However, despite all the advantages of clinical legal education, moving to an entirely clinical model for the third year of law school is probably not the panacea that some seem to believe it to be.

The first concern that rears its head again is cost. To be effective, clinical education has to be accomplished in small classes with low student/faculty ratios. This is expensive and is the primary reason that, in most law schools only about a quarter of each graduating class is able to have an experience in their school's clinic.[157] In addition, while some 3L students may be thought to be "wasting" the year, there are many others who are taking courses on subjects they need (and want) to be exposed to. Others are able to take seminars giving them close contact with their professors, and the attendant increased feedback. Often 3Ls work part time in law firms in the towns where they go to school, and in many cases, these provide many of the benefits of a clinical experience. So while it would be unquestionably valuable for more students in more law schools to have a clinical experience, simply switching the 3L year to an all clinical model alone may not be the solution. This is true for a reason found in the different nature of what law students and medical students study.

The goals of medical education and legal education differ significantly, and this difference is driven primarily by the nature of the subject matter. The "target" of medical education is the human body, which does not vary much except when it malfunctions. The "target" of legal education is human interaction, which is subject to almost infinite

---

[157] Michelle Weyenberg, *Best in Practical Training*, NAT'L JURIST, Sept. 2008, at 28.

variation. Once medical students understand the "book learning" of how the circulatory system works (for example), what they need most is to be exposed to the variability within that system, and so the clinical model for the last two years of medical education is exactly right. When they are awarded an M.D. degree, they still need more clinical education. But over time they become experts in the system (heart, skin, bones, etc.) of their choice within the human body, and then usually spend the rest of their careers specializing in that sub-system of what is essentially a closed system.

The legal system is not closed in any way. Indeed, it is constantly changing with the daily addition of new statutes, rules, regulations, and so on.[158] So the goals of legal education are in a sense more modest than medical education: to equip graduates with a basic understanding of how the legal system works, how to find answers, how to express those answers, how to perform essential lawyering skills, and how to adjust what they have learned to what they see. These are goals that — by the very nature of the extraordinary variability of the subject matter — make it certain law schools will always fall short of the sort of mastery of a limited area that medical education is able to accomplish in the clinical setting. In other words, extrapolating the interviewing skills learned in a social security matter to the skills needed to interview an expert in a complex environmental case works to a point, but only to a point. In sum, more clinical experiences in law studies, especially in the 3L year, would certainly have benefits, but it is not the entire answer.

The Integration Problem

A better approach would be to seriously address the suggestion in the 2007 Carnegie Report and infuse as many casebook classes as possible with practical applications of what is being studied. But a greater integration between the casebook courses and the practical applications of what is learned there runs into at least two significant barriers that

---

[158] Of course, it is acknowledged that several fields in medicine have wide variability in them, perhaps none more so than infectious diseases. This comparison between educational "targets" is not a perfect one. Indeed, it is offered as more true than less true, but not exact by any means.

prevent it from happening to a significant degree, at least today. The first, described in more detail in Chapter 4, is that faculty members at most law schools are ill-equipped to teach in this way. They are theorists and so theory is what they teach. They are not practicing attorneys and so practice is not what they teach. The second significant barrier is that it is too complicated. That is, it is already hard enough to cover the material in a Contracts or Torts class. To add yet another layer on top of what is already taught in these courses is perceived as too difficult, or too intrusive of the core material of the course.

In addition to these major barriers, there are some minor barriers to the integration solution. Number one is that materials needed to teach in a more practical way are hard to come by and require too many resources to develop on one's own (and there are few incentives to do so). A second is that the casebooks the legal publishers publish do not support integrated teaching of the subjects they cover. Third, it is too difficult to coordinate the complexities of live simulations. And fourth, the large class sizes (usually in the core subject courses) do not lend themselves to this sort of instruction.

Fortunately, the application of technology in ways we have already seen, and in new ways we have not seen yet, can go a long way towards breaking down these barriers in the future. Similar barriers exist in secondary education and at the college level as well. The recent report from the U.S. Department of Education suggests this is changing already at those levels: "We see dramatic changes taking place in the educational landscape — a new excitement in the vast possibilities of the digital age for changing how we learn, how we teach, and how the various segments of our educational system fit together — a ferment for reform that is bringing changes undreamt of even five years ago and unparalleled in our nation's history."[159]

The Application of Technology to Legal Education

As we have seen, the criticisms of legal education — which go primarily to the need for more individualized

---

[159] TECHNOLOGY PLAN, *supra* note 18, at 9.

instruction of a more skills and ethics oriented curriculum — has been advocated for decades, and yet little has changed. The reason is primarily cost-driven. The cost of a legal education has already soared in the last 15 years, and more individualized instruction would only cost more. And so we return to the stalemate, with competing forces pushing against each other, essentially leaving both at a standstill. The thesis of this book is that technology will, gradually, break the impasse. There are many ways in which it will do this.

As was described in Chapter 7, online technologies have now matured to the point where they can support near-classroom experiences and do so in a cost-effective way. This opens the possibility of some classes meeting online, and others meeting in the classroom, and both happening in the same course. In a first year torts class, for example, the 90 or so students in the class could meet physically in the classroom in thirds. That is, a third of the class could meet together on the first class period of the week, while the second third could meet on the second period, and so on. The remaining two thirds of the class periods could be conducted online, with a video podcast or a streaming video of the lecture, with a series of forum discussions to extend the material, and a self-assessing quiz to reinforce it. Breaking the large classes down to roughly 30 students would go a long way toward preserving one of the major cost factors in law school (the leveraging of many students to one professor) and yet also address the need for more individualized, small group instruction.

Further, if there is less need for classroom time to "cover the material," then classroom time could be used for more valuable purposes, such as contextual and experiential learning exercises. Some professors would balk at the idea that they would have to give up precious time in the classroom. But they should really welcome this model since in it the professor becomes *more* of a facilitator of learning in the classroom and less a mere dispenser of knowledge.

It remains a considerable concern that, in particular, third year students are disengaging from the traditional law school classroom. But student response systems ("clickers") can improve their engagement in class and provide a self-assessed and self-motivated method of learning. However, clickers need to be used in creative ways which advance the learning objective, not simply for an automatically graded quiz.

We are only beginning to address the question of how to effectively take advantage of laptops in the classroom. But if teachers were engaged with their students in using the power of the laptop in a way that advanced the students' learning, the concern about misuse of the laptop would vanish. There is so much that a laptop can do to enable more and better learning. The best ways to do this will be specific, of course, to the subjects we teach, so we have to go to the trouble of examining how to best integrate the tool into our objectives for that course.

Wikis and blogs have myriad applications to law school learning, particularly when the goal is to encourage collaborative work and mutual discovery. As the Carnegie 2007 report notes, a significant goal of law school is to indoctrinate students into a community of practice. Involving practitioners in a class wiki or blog allows that to happen far more regularly than it can in a typical classroom.

Something that is only beginning to be explored in legal education is the role that online gaming can play in learning. There is a Discovery game written by Owen Fiss, a professor at Yale which is distributed by CALI - the Center for Computer Aided Legal Instruction. This game simulates the discovery battle in a mock litigation and it shows much promise for this sort of learning. There is other promising work being conducted in Scotland by law professor Paul Maharg,[160] who over the past several years has developed a large multi-player game that simulates a complex legal dispute in a virtual online world. Professor Maharg's virtual world includes a town, the people who live in it, law offices that represent different people, and many documents for the students to review and help create. The Daniel Webster Scholar's Program at Franklin Pierce Law School has plans to use some of Maharg's work to extend their program beyond the 15 students per year it currently serves.

Such simulations show great potential for many applications in law school pedagogy. But one in particular is the

---

[160] http://zeugma.typpad.com/zeugma (last visited October 4, 2008).

extension of our clinics. Often clinics only reach a portion of the law school community. Through these sorts of online virtual clinic experiences more students could have access to this sort of experiential learning.

If we can use the technology to better prepare our students for the practice they are going into — and in new and creative ways — our teaching will be more relevant to them, and we will have fewer concerns about the high cost of the degree since we will be providing greater value.

The Connection Between Autonomy and Technology

Hidden in the Humanizing Movement's call for more autonomy support for our students is the same conundrum we have already seen in the other criticisms of legal education. To encourage students' initiative and self-direct-edness requires in the main more practical courses, lower student-faculty ratios, greater numbers of small classes, and more one-on-one feedback. Worse, it could lead to a downgrade of a law school's ranking by reducing a hiring emphasis on scholarship. We return to the stalemate where change is not likely to happen. But here again technology can make the difference by bridging these gaps.

It should be obvious, of course, that denying students their laptops in class threatens their autonomy in a fairly direct fashion. A more detailed discussion of the laptop debate is found in Chapter 6, but now we simply need to remind ourselves that we now have on hand a generation of students for whom technology is second nature, and for whom it is a platform for expression and self determination.

Beyond the laptop debate, there is a strong connection between autonomy support and the many technologies that are now maturing for law school teaching described in other parts of this book. A law school that encourages group work — online learning, increased engagement in learning, and connections to the practical requirements of contemporary law practice — must by definition be one that is leveraging technology to accomplish that. If a law school is serious about supporting the autonomy of its students, most of whom are part of a generation that is used to working collaboratively online and learning in hypertextual ways, it should begin to reduce (or abandon) the efforts to control its students' separateness that have been so much a part of traditional legal education. As has been noted, the Millennial Generation is one that values collaboration and co-creation in the use of online tools. Instead of treating them like individual vessels for our learning, perhaps we should also be rewarding them for collaborating effectively. While there is a role in law school for individual memorization of core concepts and structures, perhaps this role should take a back seat to deeper analysis and creative processing of legal information, especially because this is what they will need most for the law practice of the future.

The grade pressure of law school primarily supports the "sorting function" of law schools that our students' future employers seem to value. But while these employers say they want the "best" students, what they may be getting when they focus on grades only are the most effective rote memorizers. Given the changes in business and the legal profession of the last decades, it remains to be seen if that is what the employers of our students will need in the future. Better might be also awarding grades for the best collaborators, for the most ingenious, the most creative among them — in addition to the usual measurements of their facility with the basic structures of the law and legal expression — since this might just be the sorting function that employers will need more in the future. We would then have an educational environment which would value the initiative and self-directedness of our students, and would also increase their autonomy and engagement in learning. This would certainly produce healthier law students and, ultimately, healthier lawyers. Opening ourselves and our classrooms to the possibilities of technology to provide platforms for this sort of learning is an essential step.

As part of this opening ourselves to new possibilities, we should make it our business to be aware of new, emerging technologies as they appear. An example would be a new pair of them just coming over the horizon that have been given the rather antic names of digg and del.icio.us. Both support common bookmarking and community sharing of items of news or information on the web. Such technologies could be used in law school as part of an online wiki-based learning exercise in which members of the class are essentially "voting" on the best and most useful contributions to the collaborative learning exercise, and thus improving it over time.

The Skills-Focused Legal Textbook

As has been noted, the primary method of instruction in law school classrooms is through the case method, and this method typically uses a casebook. A casebook is really not a textbook, but rather a collection of appellate cases interspersed with notes and questions. Through reading and discussion of these cases students gradually learn not only how to "think like a lawyer" but also the outlines of the doctrine in the area of law being studied. Admiringly able and even necessary as this pedagogy is, it can be quite out of touch with the actual practice of law since lawyers — even litigators — rarely go to trial, and appellate cases are the exception, not the norm, for most practitioners. The strength of the casebook is in the "thinking" teaching, not the "doing" teaching. But since this is the most common form of law school teaching, legal publishers go on producing traditional casebooks and to date there has been little market for anything different.

One of the biggest impediments therefore to the adoption of a more practice-centered pedagogy is the lack of books with which to teach in this new way. Sure, most law professors would be able to develop teaching materials that would provide a practice context to what is being learned and many do. But it takes extra work and there is very little incentive to do this work in the current reward structure of law school teaching. It is thus critical if change is to occur to have textbooks that are more practice oriented in their design and approach.

In fact, textbooks of this sort are being developed. They contain problem sets that students can work on either with the teacher, in work groups, or on their own. And they support self-assessing tools that allow students to receive feedback on how they are doing throughout the course. The problem sets provide practice oriented contexts for what is being learned in the traditional casebook, and enforce and clarify what is contained there. And the best ones will include simulations of ethical dilemmas that attorneys who practice in each course's area regularly face and which will ask the student to work their way to a resolution of the ethical concerns. These textbooks will lend themselves most effectively to the hybrid textbook model, where the portions of the text that need to be in print will be in print, and the portions that can be more effective online will be online. These are hopeful, positive developments and the sooner the new casebooks become available the better.

The Evolution of the Law Review

One of the more interesting questions about the future of legal education is what will happen to the traditional law review. These journals of legal scholarship, typically selected and edited by the highest-ranking second and third year students in law schools across the country, have been a mainstay of legal education for more than a century. Every law school has at least one such journal, and most have more than one. But law reviews are threatened by the web, since authors can simply self-publish their work and bypass the need for student editing and approval, something that has for years caused grumbling among legal scholars. Indeed, a website has come onto the scene in the last few years to collect and disseminate legal scholarship (and other disciplines as well) called the Social Science Research Network (SSRN). In just a few years, tens of thousands of scholarly papers have been published on SSRN. But notably, many of those papers have also been published in traditional law journals.

And therein lies the likely result. Law reviews will always provide a level of "certification" that will remain valuable in the world of legal education. And the careful editing and footnoting that the student editors do provides considerable value as well. But all law reviews should have an online component and have a place where they can publish work before it is issued in print and where some articles can be published only online. These sites could host blogs for discussion of the scholarship published in both the print and online versions of the journal. Print will do what print does well, and online will do what only online can do — be more interactive and current.

The Future of our Learning Spaces

Another important concern for legal education in the future involves our spaces for learning. Most law schools still primarily have the traditional large classrooms they have had for decades. In these classrooms, all students face the teacher, who stands in a central well with a podium from which to speak. For legal education to change and grow in the next decades, we not only need to employ technology more creatively, but also reconfigure many of our learning spaces. Large classrooms were appropriate for the time when information was scarce. But information is no longer scarce, indeed it is easily available and abundant. As a result, we need to create spaces that are more about learning than they are about the mere transfer of information, that is, spaces that foster collaboration and value learning over rote instruction. At least some of the traditional large rooms in most law schools could and should be reconfigured to create smaller "socially catalytic spaces" that support innovation and experimentation.[161] These smaller rooms could have round tables, for example, and the teacher could move around while using different media and methods to foster interaction.

The Digital Literacy Problem

As we have seen, the often stated goal of legal education is to teach students to "think like a lawyer." But of course that should be only the first goal. The second should be to show law students how to conduct research, that is, to learn like a lawyer. And the third skill should be to teach law students to learn how to learn. We have a responsibility to teach our students to be excellent life-long learners because that is, more than anything else, what the practice of law requires. Professor Michael Wesch at Kansas State University has noted that our students may know how to use online collaborative technologies and may have used them in their personal lives for several years, but they do not necessarily

---

[161] DIANA G. OBLINGER, LEARNING SPACES, 142 (2006).

know how to use them for learning. This means that we have a duty to our students to make sure that we teach them how to use these tools effectively and efficiently, and especially how to use them to learn and to become life-long learners in a primarily digital world.

Professor Stuart Selber of Penn State University has written about digital literacy in the undergraduate context. He explains that there really are three types of digital literacy, functional, critical, and rhetorical, and that all three forms are essential aspects of any program that professes to be both valuable and professionally responsible.[162]

Selber's Three Forms of Digital Literacy

• Functional
    o   How the technology works
 	
• Critical
    o   How the technology affects what is being studied
 	
• Rhetorical
    o   How to use the technology to create

Functional literacy is how the thing works. Critical literacy is being able to think of how the thing affects what is being studied. And rhetorical literacy is about knowing how to create with the thing. Selber notes that students require "direct, repeated, and integrated contact with the particulars of all three literacies in order to become well-rounded individuals equipped with a keen and judicious sense of the technological world around them."[163]

This means not only that we must integrate technology into our teaching, but we must also realize that our students do not necessarily know how to use these tools for learning. We must intentionally teach them not only the function, but also broader aspects of how the technology affects the world around them, and how to use the tools to effectively practice law in the future.

---

[162] STUART SELBER, MULTILITERACIES FOR A DIGITAL AGE (2004).

[163] Stuart A. Selber, Assistant Professor of English at Penn State University, Keynote Address at the University of Denver Technology and the Human Mind Conference (Apr. 27, 2007).

The Skills Teachers

As we envision a legal education that emphasizes the increased autonomy of the student, the importance of teaching of legal skills, and the use of new and innovative technologies and learning spaces, the question arises: who in the legal academy can teach in this way? The answer is that a cadre of teachers capable of this new sort of pedagogy already exists in the legal academy. These are most especially the legal skills and legal writing teachers who are usually the most innovative and pedagogy-focused teachers in today's law schools. These professors have the advantage of teaching in smaller classes where they can experiment with all manner of technological tools and refine their uses. In time the larger faculty can adopt the best of what these skills teachers have found effective. In short, these skills teachers serve as catalysts in their law schools, but, very importantly, they need to be given credit for the role they play and appropriate security in their positions. The legal academy simply has to get over the old caste system in law faculties, because good skills teachers are vital to the developing future of legal education. They have to be valued and protected or they will go elsewhere. This is starting to be addressed, but it needs to accelerate.

Some have suggested that the answer to the change/cost conundrum is to hire more adjunct faculty to teach the skills courses. Because adjunct faculty members are comparatively inexpensive to hire and they work on their practice skills every day, that may seem like an attractive solution. But hiring more adjunct faculty is not the right answer, for several reasons. First, many law schools already rely heavily on adjunct faculty, and some of them are in danger of running afoul of ratios between adjunct and full-time faculty that are a required part of the ABA accreditation process. Second, adjuncts make many valuable contributions to legal educa- tion, but they are rarely overseen, their primary loyalty is to their practices (as it must be) and the quality can be uneven as a result. Third, adjunct faculty members are not part of faculty governance for the institution they serve in any way, and rarely have much interaction with the full-time faculty. Fourth, if we assign adjunct faculty the responsibility to teach all of our skills courses, we have not addressed the criticism that we should include more skills teaching throughout all law school courses, we have merely abdicated it to someone else and off to other courses. Fifth, leveraging pedagogical technology as contemplated in this book takes time and effort, and few practitioners have the time to learn how to teach the law in this way. Finally, if we assign adjunct faculty to teach these courses, we are merely perpetuating the same problems that lead us to where we are today — by not admitting and accepting the responsibility to teach the law in a new way.

Of course, adjunct faculty members play a valuable and important role in many law schools. They bring subject-matter expertise that may be lacking on the full-time faculty, and teach such courses for little compensation, and often in the evening hours. However, because the need for skills and practice-focused teaching is so deep and broad in legal education, simply assigning the "dirty work" to members of the adjunct faculty will make little progress towards effectuating significant change in legal education.

The law school of the future will rest on a three legged stool with research faculty, clinical faculty and legal process skills faculty each playing a different but equally critical role in the education of our students. While some might think there is a potential conflict between clinical and legal process skills faculty, there should not be. Skills faculty should be thought of as providing a base level of skills to all students, and preparing those who want a clinical experience to leverage what they have learned so they are ready to excel in the clinic when they get there. There should in fact be more skills courses, but the skills courses are also the ideal places for pedagogical innovation to take root and grow.

Further Reading

Diana G. Oblinger, Learning Spaces (2006).

Clayton M. Christensen et al., Disrupting Class: How Disruptive Innovation Will Change the Way the World Learns (2008).

Stuart A. Selber, Multiliteracies for a Digital Age (2004).

Paul Maharg, Transforming Legal Education: Learning and Teaching the Law in the Early Twenty-First Century (2007).

CONCLUSION

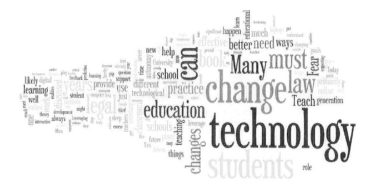

We are in a period of deep ferment in legal education. Many of its failings and some of its successes are being closely examined and widely discussed. Left out of this discussion almost entirely is the role technology can and will play in changing legal education for the better. Many law schools are instituting some quite radical educational reforms, but there seems to be little coherence among them and no explicit role for technology. Professor Larry Krieger recently wrote: "When broad changes are contemplated, as in the current education community, it is wise and most efficient to first adopt a deep theory to provide consistent guidance and ensure coherent, well-reasoned change."[164] But while we are working towards a "deep theory," there is virtually no discussion or understanding of the role that technology can play in developing such a theory. It is critical that it be considered and analyzed appropriately as we discuss and

---

[164] Lawrence S. Krieger, HUMAN NATURE AS A NEW GUIDING PHILOSOPHY FOR LEGAL EDUCATION AND THE PROFESSION, 47 WASHBURN L.J. 247, 310 (2008).

develop changes in legal education. This is true primarily for four reasons:

We must Teach them Appropriately: This generation of students is familiar with using technology to support their learning and this is a trend that will only increase. It is essentially invisible to them, and it works. It brings them benefits students have never had before. For most things (although not all) our students have short attention spans, primarily because they are saturated in a fast moving stream of media every day of their lives. They are used to collaborative work, and they believe that it works (because, done right, it does). Given these facts, the days of lecturing behind a podium for a full class period are over, or they soon will be. It just does not work well. It arguably never did, but it certainly will not for these students. Technology can help us provide information to our students in ways they are used to receiving it, thus leading to increased engagement. We have to explore and become proficient in opening up our class periods to group work and other teaching methods that leverage technology, and we have to find the time and the methods to provide more feedback to our students. We must learn about, and use, the increasingly available and effective tools for delivering some of our course content in an online environment. We all want to be good and effective teachers of our students. We simply have to teach them in a way that leverages their comfort with technology and collaborative work. It is only appropriate that we do so.

We must Teach them Accurately: The practice of law has been changing in significant ways for the past 30 years. Most of these changes have accelerated in the last 15 years, many of them driven by technology. These changes are not just a matter of inputting your time slips into a computer instead of writing them down for a secretary to transcribe as lawyers used to do. Today attorneys usually prepare their own documents in word processing software, and in many jurisdictions they are required to file their documents electronically. They research primarily online now, and they use complex programs such as CaseMap to manage cases and other client matters. Electronic discovery in litigation is just one example of how pervasive, and important, a deep understanding of technology (and how it affects client realities) is now for our graduates. They are faced in practice today with data sets of a magnitude that have never existed before. The question of the level of digital literacy our graduates will need for practice is barely discussed in law schools today. But developments in technology are driving many of the changes that are happening in the legal profession. Our students must be prepared for this reality.

We must Teach them Humanely: The evidence is mounting that the old "Kingsfield" model of legal education is not only counter-productive for this generation, but that it may have been actually causing *harm* to our students. And there are many things that we can do to increase the autonomy support that our students need, from administration, staff and faculty, in and out of the classroom. One of the best and most effective things we can do is to integrate technology into our teaching and our various interactions with our students. Leveraging the interactive capabilities of technology to reach this generation can go a long way toward supporting the autonomy of our students. Complaining about their laptops in the classroom is a negative influence in terms of supporting their autonomy. We must instead engage in learning how to employ all available technology for the betterment of their learning. This will be hard work. It demands that we learn how to be better, more effective teachers. It also means we must change our incentive structure in law schools to support this work. If we do not make these adjustments, we risk gradually becoming less and less effective teachers, and we even run the risk of harming our students. Eventually students will rebel. It would be much better to get in front of this curve.

We must Teach them Properly: The complaints about legal education have been essentially the same for decades. Generally, they all sing the same tune: law schools must play a bigger role in bridging the gap between law school and legal practice. For many years the common and effective answer to that suggestion has been: we cannot afford it. But that is no longer true. With technology we can leverage our most expensive resources, namely our faculties, in new and creative ways. We have already started to do this, albeit in baby steps. Many faculty members now put certain basic information online. But we should use quizzes that are designed to teach and give instant feedback, as well as provide assessment. Textbooks need not cost as much as they do and they will not if only portions of them are printed and the rest is provided in an interactive, online format. We will need to learn how to use and teach from these hybrid textbooks. Technology can help us to provide information to our students in ways that they will need to know - to properly receive, interpret, and manage it in practice.

If we can make these changes, our teaching will be more effective, providing our students with more feedback and fostering greater interaction between student and teacher. It is not too expensive anymore. We just have to learn how to leverage the technology we have, and be open to possibilities for a type of teaching we may have not considered before. Our students increasingly are experiencing these sorts of applications of educational technology in high school and college. If they arrive in law school and our instructional methods remain primarily in the 1890s, we can expect them to tune out. Indeed, by third year many of them already have. It is urgent that we use that third year of law school in particular to help them bridge the gap between law school and the realities of the practice of law they are about to enter. At present we are not using any of the three years of law school optimally to help them bridge the gap and we are nearly wasting the third year.

The Question of When

At one point or another, anyone who has the audacity to try to make predictions about the future is always asked, usually quite urgently, "when?" As in, "Maybe we believe you. But if so, when is this all going to happen?" The answer in the case of legal education reform is, of course, impossible to give. Further, it will not occur at a precise point in time, but rather will be a gradual progression extending over a period of as much as 10 or 20 years.

The story of the development of the zipper is once again instructive. It took 45 years for the zipper to be perfected, to be accepted into general use and to become universal — to reach critical mass. If our starting point is the development of the Internet as a platform for many of the changes to legal education discussed in this book, we are only 10 years into this process.

Of course, technological change has, for the most part, sped up dramatically in recent decades. Computer technology in particular has driven change at an even quicker pace. In a famous essay published in 2001, "Law of Accelerating Returns," the technologist Ray Kurzweil wrote of this speed-up. One of the best-known examples Kurzweil addresses is Moore's law, which posited that the number of transistors on a computer chip would double every two years. Since Gordon Moore made that prediction in 1965, it has become approximately true. In his essay, Kurzweil extends Moore's law and posits that technological change has become exponential in more ways than just the number of transistors that can be fit onto a silicon chip. This suggests, of course, that significant, technological, cultural, and pedagogical changes such as those discussed in this book could happen faster than we think.

Still, it would be wise to remember that despite the speed of technological change and the advantages it may offer to teachers, we are talking about a complex human system that has been largely unaltered for 100 years. The foundations of legal education are sunk deep and shaking them may take longer than we think despite the Law of Accelerating Returns. Change will not come overnight, but more likely will be gradual, incremental, and locally determined; and will be managed in different ways along many different paths. After all, as Professor Freidel noted in his book about the zipper: "In technological change, as in much of life, results come neither from technical and cultural imperatives nor from individual and institutional will, but from the constant interaction of these elements."[165]

This book is not intended to be a roadmap or a prescription, but an opening to the possibilities, and to encourage experimentation with them. There is no list of technology each classroom must have, or a list of what teachers must learn. The answers will be different for each school, for each institutional culture, and will need to be designed to achieve different educational goals and serve

---

[165] FRIEDEL, ZIPPER, *supra* note 95, at ix.

different constituencies. In other words, it will likely happen at each school differently, and on a different timeline.

The Question of Fear

For many members of the legal academy, what is described in this book will sound like a radical upending of the order of things between teacher and student. It is not. It is about doing what we do best, only doing it better. It is about adding new skills to those we already have so that we may connect better with our students, and teach them things they will need to know for the changing law practice of the future.

Many will also feel that what is described in this book sounds like a dramatic shift in the primacy of the university system in legal education. It is not that either. Five years ago John Chambers, the CEO of Cisco Systems, said: "In five years, the university will be dead." Not only was he clearly wrong, but such a prediction is silly. We will always need the "certification" of the university. And we will always need the university to be a safe place for inquiry and challenge. Law schools are no exception to this.

We do need, however, to stop acting primarily in our own self-interest, to act more as fiduciaries of the sacred and essential place that our collective legal academy holds in our society. Yes, we might have to put in some extra effort. Yes, to a large extent we must all embrace the change, knowing there is nothing to fear but our own irrelevance.

Often the source of the fear is radical change — the fear, for example, that digital books will completely replace something we intimately understand, the physical book. The fear comes from the prospect that something we deeply understand how to use will go away and be replaced by something we do not know how to use. But technology rarely brings this sort of radical change — it is more often additive. That is, the digital book will have its uses and benefits, but there will remain plenty of room for physical books to do what they do well. Once we see that technology brings new capabilities more often than it destroys old ones we can be less afraid of it.

Incentives can be put in place to soften the fear, and instruction and assistance can help as well. We need administrators who understand this and are willing to support it. And we must start focusing on outputs and embrace reliable assessment methods. If we are not willing to be accurately measured on our success in achieving the educational goals of our law schools, we might as well give up teaching.

The Futility of Resistance

Lastly, it seems pointless to resist these sorts of changes, since in one way or another, they will happen everywhere eventually. Technology is an unstoppable force. Many developments are coming together at the same time — our changing students, maturing technological tools for education, the various studies that have pushed hard for reforms in legal education. As the Department of Education report noted, "these changes are being driven by forces in the field. They are being driven by the new realities of the digital marketplace, the rapid development of "virtual" schools, and the enthusiasm of an amazing generation of students weaned on the marvels of technology who are literally forcing our schools to adapt and change in ways never before imagined."[166]

To reduce the thesis of this book into one thought picture, visualize this: the calls for change in legal education look like a disorganized pile of dry firewood. The kindling is in place underneath the wood, and the crumpled newspaper waits expectantly. If the forces of resistance to change again push out or compromise these reforms, the wood will continue to dry and crack, but nothing significant will happen. The wood will be useless and will provide no warmth. This book has attempted to describe how technology can, finally, be the match.

Technology is the match — or the point on which change will pivot — for four primary reasons: 1) It enhances student engagement, if used properly. 2) It helps us reach our expanding educational goals inexpensively and more efficiently. 3) It reaches this generation more effectively, by being more personal, and supporting student autonomy

---

[166] TECHNOLOGY PLAN, *supra* note 18, at 10.

better than the authoritarian approach to teaching. And 4) it better prepares our students for the practice in which they will spend their professional lives. Without leveraging technology, we cannot achieve these goals. Technology *facilitates* the changes discussed in this book, because it can help to create relevant, interactive, active learning experiences in and out of the classroom. Technology *lubricates* the changes discussed in this book because it can loosen some of the economic barriers to change, such as leveraging economies of scale, enabling more online learning, and helping to maximize our most precious resource: our faculties.

References

Chapter 2: The Perfect Storm

John Thompson, *Is Education 1.0 Ready for Web 2.0 Students?*, 3 INNOVATE (2007), *available at* http://www.innovateonline.info/index.php?view=article&id=393.

Arden L. Bement, *Cyberinfrastructure: the Second Revolution*, 53 CHRON. HIGHER EDUC. (Wash., D.C.), Jan. 5, 2007, at B5.

Joseph Berger, *Classroom of the Future Is Virtually Anywhere*, N.Y. TIMES, October 31, 2007, at A22.

Leary Davis, *Creating a National Model for Legal Education at Elon — and Why*, N.C. STATE BAR J., Winter 2006, at 14.

Elaine McArdle, *A Curriculum of New Realities: At Harvard Law School, some new answers to the question, What do future lawyers need to know?*, HARV. L. BULL., Winter 2008, at 18.

Parker J. Palmer, *A New Professional: The Aims of Education Revisited*, CHANGE Nov./Dec. 2007, *available at* http://www.carnegiefoundation.org/change/sub.asp?key=98&sub-key=2455&printable=true.

Eric Alterman, *Out of Print*, NEW YORKER, Mar. 31, 2008, at 48.

Chris Anderson, *Why $0.00 is the Future of Business*, WIRED, Mar. 2008, at 140.

M. Mitchell Waldrop, *Science 2.0*, SCI. AM., May 2008, at 69.

Elia Powers, *Being Active (Or Not) in Law School,* Inside Higher Education, (January 3, 2008) *available at* http://www.inside-highered.com/news/2008/01/03/lssse

Katherine Mangan, *Legal Educators Respond to Proposed Curriculum Changes with Enthusiasm and Skepticism*, CHRON. HIGHER EDUC. (Wash., D.C.), Jan. 7, 2008, *available at* http://chronicle.com/temp/email2.php?id=rYtKJJ4-hyrxsCmnwkkjp8zKZNHjhzb5R.

James Gleick, *Keeping It Real: Why, in an age of free information, would anyone pay millions for a document?*, N.Y. TIMES MAG., Jan. 6, 2008, at 13.

Frank Rich, *The Grand Old White Party Confronts Obama*, N.Y. TIMES, Feb. 17, 2008, at 13.

Steve Lohr, *Study Says Computers Give Big Boosts to Productivity*, N.Y. TIMES, March 13, 2008, at C4.

Chapter 3: The Millennial Generation

Robin A. Boyle, *Generation X in Law School: How these Law Students are Different from those who Teach Them*, 56 J. LEGAL EDUC. 281 (2006).

Damon Darlin, *Technology Doesn't Dumb Us Down. It Frees Our Minds.*, N.Y. TIMES, Sept. 21, 2008 at BU 4.

HENRY JENKINS ET AL., MACARTHUR FOUND., CONFRONTING THE CHALLENGES OF PARTICIPATORY CULTURE: MEDIA EDUCATION FOR THE 21ST CENTURY (2006).

Nicholas Carr, *Is Google Making Us Stoopid?*, ATLANTIC, July/Aug. 2008, at 63, *available at* http://www.theatlantic.com/doc/200807/google.

John Lanchester, *Log On. Tune Out: Lee Siegel looks at the way the Internet is reshaping American culture — and doesn't like what he sees*, N.Y. TIMES BOOK REV., Feb. 3, 2008, at 10.

Virginia Heffernan, *My Wired Youth: Coming of age online — 25 years ago — was more and less than a game*, N.Y. TIMES MAG., Feb. 3, 2008, at 20.

Stephanie Rosenbloom, *Generation Me vs. You Revisited*, N.Y. TIMES, Jan. 17, 2008, at E6.

Jeff Leeds, *Radiohead Finds Sales, Even After Downloads*, N.Y. TIMES, Jan. 10, 2008, at B1.

Claudia Dreifus, *In Professor's Model, Diversity = Productivity*, N. Y. TIMES, Jan. 8, 2008, at D2.

Caleb Crain, *Twilight of the Books: What will life be like if people stop reading?*, NEW YORKER, Dec. 24, 2007, at 139.

Michelle Slatalla, *Today, I Think I'll Be Hippohead*, N.Y. TIMES, May 8, 2008, at E2.

Steven D. Schwinn, Developmental Learning Theory in the First Year: From Regression to Progression, (May 25, 2008) *available at*: http://papers.ssrn.com/sol3/papers.cfm?abstract_id=1137047

Louis Rossetto, Good thing we got some stuff right: 2. We foresaw the One Machine, WIRED, May 19, 2008, at 175.

Ian Gallacher, 2007, *"Who Are Those Guys?:" The Results of a Survey Studying the Information Literacy of Incoming Law Students*, 44 CAL. W. L. REV. (forthcoming) *available at*: http://papers.ssrn.com/sol3/papers.cfm?abstract_id=1004088

James B. Levy, *A Schema Walks into a Bar ... How Humor Makes Us Better Teachers by Helping Our Students Learn*, 16 PERSP.: TEACHING LEGAL RESEARCH & WRITING 109 (2008).

Tom Kimbraugh, *In-Class Online Legal Research Exercises: A Valuable Education Tool*, 16 PERSP.: TEACHING LEGAL RESEARCH & WRITING 112 (2008).

MICHAEL CONNERY, YOUTH TO POWER, HOW TODAY'S YOUNG VOTERS ARE BUILDING TOMORROW'S PROGRESSIVE MAJORITY (2008).

Michiko Kakutani, *Why Knowledge and Logic Are Politically Dirty Words*, N.Y. TIMES, Mar. 11, 2008, at B7.

Anthony Tommasini, *A Patience to Listen, Alive and Well*, N.Y. TIMES, Dec. 30, 2007, at AR27.

Janet Rae-Dupree, *Innovative Minds Don't Think Alike*, N.Y. TIMES, Dec. 30, 2007, at BU3.

G. Pascal Zachary, *The Risk of Innovation: Will Anyone Embrace It?*, N.Y. TIMES, Jan. 20, 2008, at BU4.

Michelle Slatalla, *If You Can't Let Go, Twitter*, N.Y. TIMES, Feb. 14, 2008, at E1.

Walter Kirn, *The Autumn of the Multitaskers*, ATLANTIC, Nov. 2007, at 66, *available at* http://www.theatlantic.com/doc/prem/2007711/multitasking.

Eric A. DeGroff, *Learning Like Lawyers: Addressing the Differences in Law Student Learning Styles*, 2006 B.Y.U. EDUC. & L.J. 499.

Walter Kirn, *The Couch Potato Path to a Higher I.Q.*, N.Y. TIMES BOOK REV., May 22, 2005, at 13.

Mike Madison, *Sharing, YouTube, and the Law School Community, Law & Technology*, MADISONIAN.NET, Mar. 19, 2008, http://madisonian.net/archives/2007/03/19/sharing-youtube-and-the-law-school-community/.

Steven Johnson, *The Long Zoom*, N.Y. TIMES MAG., Oct. 8, 2006, at 50.

Eric Kelderman, *Legislators barring electronic distractions*, STATELINE.ORG, Feb. 22, 2007, http://www.stateline.org/live/details/story?contentId=182728.

Lori Aratani, *Teens Can Multitask, But What Are Costs? Ability to Analyze May Be Affected, Experts Worry*, WASH. POST, Feb. 26, 2007 at A01, *available at* http://www.washingtonpost.com/wp-dyn/content/article/2007/02/25/AR2007022501600_pf.html.

HARVARD UNIV. INSTIT. OF POLITICS, THE 11TH BIANNUAL YOUTH SURVEY ON POLITICS AND PUBLIC SERVICE 3, 9 (2006).

Center for Information Behaviour and the Evaluation of Research (CIBER), University College London, *Information Behaviour of the Researcher of the Future* (Jan. 11, 2008).

Stuart Elliot, *Telling the Heavyweights How to Avoid Extinction*, N. Y. TIMES, Apr. 30, 2008, at C6.

THE PEW RESEARCH CTR. FOR THE PEOPLE & THE PRESS, HOW YOUNG PEOPLE VIEW THEIR LIVES, FUTURES AND POLITICS: A PORTRAIT OF "GENERATION NEXT", Jan. 9, 2007.

WILLIAM STRAUSS & NEIL HOWE, MILLENNIALS GO TO COLLEGE: STRATEGIES FOR NEW GENERATION ON CAMPUS (2003).

WILLIAM STRAUSS & NEIL HOWE, MILLENNIALS RISING: THE NEXT GREAT GENERATION (2000).

GERALD F. HESS & STEVEN I. FRIEDLAND, TECHNIQUES FOR TEACHING LAW (1999).

MARK BAUERLEIN, THE DUMBEST GENERATION: HOW THE DIGITAL AGE STUPEFIES YOUNG AMERICANS AND JEOPARDIZES OUR FUTURE (OR, DON'T TRUST ANYONE UNDER 30) (2008).

Christine Rosen, *The Myth of Multitasking*, NEW ATLANTIS, Spring 2008, at 105.

Chapter 4: The Practice of Law

Mark Horowitz, *Visualizing Big Data: If We Could See Everything Ever Written At Once, How Would It Look, and What Could It Tell Us?*, WIRED, ISSUE 16.07 (July 2008) *available at* http://www.wired.com/science/discoveries/magazine/16-07/pb_visualizing.

EDWARD R. TUFTE, THE VISUAL DISPLAY OF QUANTITATIVE INFORMATION (2nd Ed. 2001).

Futurelawyer, http://futurelawyer.typepad.com/.

Rick B. Allan, *Lawyers: Are We a Profession in Distress?* NEB. LAW., Oct. 1998, at 22.

Ruth E. Piller, *Authors of Raise the Bar Hope to Do Just That*, LITIG. NEWS, Jan. 2008, at 5.

C.C. Holland, *High-Tech Catches a Juror's Eye and Mind*, LAW.COM, Feb. 12, 2008, http://www.law.com/jsp/legaltechnology/pubArticleLT.jsp?id=1202054124864.

Daphne Eviatar, *Howrey Vindaloo: Is a Back Office in India Too Exotic for the Firm's Clients?*, AM. LAW., Feb. 2008, at 22, *available at* http://www.law.com/jsp/article.jsp?id=1202732098332&rss=newswire.

Robin A. Boyle, *Applying Learning-Styles Theory in the Workplace: How to Maximize Learning-Styles Strengths to Improve Work Performance In Law Practice*, 79 ST. JOHN'S L. REV. 97 (2005).

Larry Richard, *How Your Personality Affects Your Practice: The Lawyer Types*, A.B.A. J., July 1993, at 74.

Neil Hamilton, *Professionalism Clearly Defined*, 18 PROF. LAW., Issue No. 4, at 4 (2008).

Lawyers with Depression, http://www.lawyerswithdepression.com/.

Cal. Bar Journal, *Depression Takes a Heavy Toll on Lawyers*, May 2008, http://www.calbar.ca.gov/state/calbar/calbar_cbj.jsp? sCategoryPath=/Home/Attorney%20Resources/California% 20Bar%20Journal/May2008&sCatHtmlPath=cbj/2008- 05_TH_02_Depression.html&sCatHtmlTitle=Top%20Head- lines.

Chapter 5: The Criticism of Legal Education

Adrian Vermeule, *Rethinking Langdell: Historic changes in 1L curriculum set stage for new upper-level programs of study*, HARVARD L. TODAY, Dec. 2006, http://www.law.harvard.edu/ news/today/dec_hlt_langdell.php.

ROY STUCKEY ET. AL, BEST PRACTICES FOR LEGAL EDUCATION: A VISION AND A ROADMAP (2007).

John O. Sonsteng et al., *A Legal Education Renaissance: A Practical Approach for the Twenty-First Century*, 34 WM MITCHELL L. REV. 303 (2007).

WILLIAM M. SULLIVAN ET AL., EDUCATING LAWYERS: PREPARATION FOR THE PROFESSION OF LAW 91 (2007).

SUSAN SWAIN DAICOFF, LAWYER KNOW THYSELF: A PSYCHOLOGICAL ANALYSIS OF PERSONALITY STRENGTHS AND WEAKNESSES (2004).

Lawrence S. Krieger, *Human Nature as a New Guiding Philosophy for Legal Education and the Profession*, 47 WASHBURN L.J. 247 (2008).

Lawrence S. Krieger, *Psychological Insights: Why Our Students and Graduates Suffer and What We Might Do About It*, 1 J. ASS'N LEGAL WRITING DIRECTORS 258 (2002).

Talbot D'Alemberte, *Law School in the Nineties: Talbot D'Alemberte on Legal Education*, 76 A.B.A. J. 52 (1990).

Robert MacCrate, *Yesterday, Today and Tomorrow: Building the Continuum of Legal Education and Professional Development*, 10 CLIN. L. REV. 805 (2004).

Michael Hunter Schwartz, *Teaching Law by Design: How Learning Theory and Instructional Design Can Inform and Reform Law Teaching*, 38 SAN DIEGO L. REV. 347 (2001).

Michael Hunter Schwartz, *Humanizing Legal Education: An Introduction to a Symposium Whose Time Came*, 47 WASHBURN L.J. 235 (2008).

Lawrence S Kreiger, *Does Legal Education Have Undermining Effects on Law Students? Evaluating Changes in Values, Motivation and Well-Being*, 22 BEHAV. SCI. & L. 261 (2004).

James B. Levy, *As a Last Resort, Ask the Students: What They Say Makes Someone an Effective Law Teacher*, 58 ME. L. REV. 49 (2006).

Indiana University Center for Postsecondary Research, Law School Survey of Student Engagement, *Student Engagement in Law School: Knowing Our Students* (2007), *available at* http://lssse.iub.edu/2007_Annual_Report/index.cfm.

Nancy Levit & Douglas O. Linder, *Happy Law Students, Happy Lawyers*, 58 SYRACUSE L. REV. 351 (2008).

MARJORIE SILVER, THE AFFECTIVE ASSISTANCE OF COUNSEL: PRACTICING LAW AS A HEALING PROFESSION (2007).

Robert P. Schuwerk, *The Law Professor as Fiduciary: What Duties Do We Owe to Our Students*, 45 S. TEX. L. REV. 753 app. at 809-11 (2004).

Gerald Hess, Gonzaga University School of Law, Presentation at the Humanizing Legal Education Conference/Symposium: Collaborative Course Design: Not My Course, Not Their Course, But Our Course (Oct. 20, 2007).

Susan Daicoff, Florida Coastal School of Law, Presentation at the Humanizing Legal Education Conference/Symposium: The Comprehensive Law Movement and its Relation to Humanizing Legal Education (Oct. 21, 2007).

Carol L. Wallinger, Rutgers School of Law-Camden, Presentation at the Humanizing Legal Education Conference/Symposium: From First to Final Draft: Autonomy Support in Legal Writing Class (Oct. 20, 2007).

AMERICAN BAR ASSOCIATION, LEGAL EDUCATION AND PROFESSIONAL DEVELOPMENT — AN EDUCATIONAL CONTINUUM: REPORT OF THE TASK FORCE ON LAW SCHOOLS AND THE PROFESSION: NARROWING THE GAP (1992).

Chapter 6: The March of Technology

ROBERT FRIEDEL, A CULTURE OF IMPROVEMENT: TECHNOLOGY AND THE WESTERN MILLENNIUM (2007).

Kathy M. Hessler, Case Western Reserve University School of Law, Presentation at the Humanizing Legal Education Conference/ Symposium: Structural and Pedagogical Choices (Oct. 20, 2007).

Matthew Bodie, *The Future of the Casebook: An Argument for an Open-Source Approach*, 57 J. LEGAL EDUC. 10 (2008).

Edward Wyatt, *Rise of Amazon's Reading Device Stirs Worries at Publishing Fair*, N.Y. TIMES, June 2, 2008, at B6.

Sharon Joy Ng Hale, *Being Online*, ACADEME, Nov./Dec. 2007, at 29.

Mylene Mangalindan et.al, *Technology (A Special Report): Thinking About Tomorrow*, WALL ST. J., Jan. 28, 2008, at R1, *available at* http://online.wsj.com/public/article/ SB120119369144313747.html.

Kevin Yamamoto, *Banning Laptops in the Classroom: Is It Worth the Hassle?*, 57 J.LEGAL EDUC. 477 (2007).

BECTA RESEARCH REPORT, EMERGING TECHNOLOGIES FOR LEARNING (March 2008).

THE NEW MEDIA CONSORTIUM & EDUCAUSE LEARNING INITIATIVE, THE HORIZON REPORT: 2008 EDITION (2008), *available at* http://net.educause.edu/ir/library/pdf/CSD5320.pdf

LARRY CUBAN, OVERSOLD & UNDERUSED: COMPUTERS IN THE CLASS-ROOM (2003).

Dennis A. Adams, R. Ryan Nelson & Peter A. Todd, *Perceived Usefulness, ease of use, and usage of information technology: a replication*, 16 MIS Quarterly 227 (1992).

Chapter 7: The Promise of Technology

Geoffrey Christopher Rapp, *Can You Show Me How To ... ? Reflections of a New Law Professor and Part-Time Technology Consultant on the Role of New Law Teachers as Catalysts for Change*, 58 J. LEGAL EDUC. 61 (2008).

Rogelio Lasso, *From the Paper Chase to the Digital Chase: Technology and the Challenge of Teaching to 21st Century Law Students*, 43 SANTA CLARA L. REV. 1 (2002).

Seth Schiesel, *Former Justice Promotes Web-Based Civics Lessons*, N.Y. TIMES, June 9, 2008, at B7.

Diana R. Donahoe, *Click Here, E-Scholars*, LEGAL TIMES, Sep. 3, 2007, at 28.

Diana R. Donahoe, *Laptops for Learning*, RES IPSA LOQUITUR (Fall/ Winter 2007), at 55.

Mark R. Nelson, *E-Books in Higher Education: Nearing the End of the Era of Hype?*, EDUCAUSE REV., Mar./Apr. 2008, at 40.

Edward Rothstein, *We Hold These Truths to Be User-Accessible and in Hypertext*, N.Y. TIMES, Apr. 12, 2008, at B7, *available at* http://www.nytimes.com/2008/04/12/arts/design/12libr.html?_r=1&em&ex=1208145600&en=d20503b52b6e87ab&ei=5087%0A&oref=slogin.

Participatory Media Literacy, https://www.socialtext.net/medialiteracy/index.cgi.

JEREMIAH K OWYANG ET. AL, ONLINE COMMUNITY BEST PRACTICES (2008).

David Pogue, *Gadget Fans, Take Note: An Update of Pen on Paper*, N.Y. TIMES, May 8, 2008, at C9.

Anthony Grafton, *Future Reading: Digitization and its discontents*, NEW YORKER, Nov. 5, 2007, at 50.

John Willinsky, *What open access research can do for Wikipedia*, FIRST MONDAY: PEER REVIEWED JOURNAL ON THE INTERNET (2007), http://www.firstmonday.org/issues/issue12_3/willinsky/index.html.

Franklyn Prescod & Linying Dong, *Learning Style Trends and Laptop Use Patterns: Implication for Students in an IT Business School*, 23 PROC ISECON § 3543 (2006).

Pat-Anthony Federico, *Learning styles and student attitudes toward various aspects of network-based instruction*, 16 COMPUTERS IN HUMAN BEHAVIOR 359 (2000).

W.M. Reed et al., *Computer experience, learning style, and hypermedia navigation*, 16 COMPUTERS IN HUMAN BEHAVIOR 609 (2000).

Catherine Ross Dunham, *Stretching Toward the Future: A View of Laptop Computers from Both Sides of the Screen*, LAW TEACHER, Spring 2007, at 1.

Jill Schachner Chanen, *Profs Kibosh Students' Laptops*, A.B.A. J., Nov. 2007, at 16, *available at* http://www.abajournal.com/magazine/profs_kibosh_students_laptops/print/.

Educause Learning Initiative, *7 things you should know about Wikis*, July 2005, http://net.educause.edu/ir/library/pdf/ELI7004.pdf

Brian Lamb, *Wide Open Spaces, Wikis Ready or Not*, EDUCAUSE, Sept./Oct. 2004, at 36.

Kevin R. Parker & Joseph T. Chao, *Wiki as a Teaching Tool*, 3 INTERDISCIPLINARY J. E-LEARNING & LEARNING OBJECTS 57 (2007), *available at* http://ijklo.org/volume3.html.

Kassandra Barnes et al., *Teaching and Learning with the Net Generation*, INNOVATAE: J. ONLINE EDUC., Apr./May 2007, *available at* http://www.innovateonline.info/index.php?view=-article&id=382

Linda B. Nilson & Barbara E. Weaver, *Enhancing Learning with Laptops in the Classroom*, NEW DIRECTIONS FOR TEACHING & LEARNING, Spring 2005, at 1.

Linda L. Briggs, *Web Technology Boosts Writing Performance at Alhambra USD*, T.H.E. J., Jan. 2008, http://www.thejournal. com/articles/21847.

Joe Nocera, *A Tight Grip Can Choke Creativity*, N.Y. TIMES, Feb. 9, 2008, at B1.

James Efaw et al., *Miracle or Menace: Teaching and Learning with Laptop Computers in the Classroom*, EDUCAUSE QUARTERLY, Fall 2004, at 10.

Michael Trimmel & Julia Bachmann, *Cognitive, Social, Motivational and Health Aspects of Students in Laptop Classrooms*, 20 J. COMPUTER ASSISTED LEARNING 151 (2004).

Jacob Hale Russell & John Jurgenson, *Fugue for Man & Machine*, WALL ST. J., May 5, 2007, at P1.

Winnie Hu, *Seeing No Progress, Some Schools Drop Laptops*, N.Y. TIMES, May 4, 2007, at A1, A23.

Maia Ridberg, *Professors want their classes "unwired"*, CHRISTIAN SCI. MONITOR, May 4, 2006, at 16, *available at* http://www. csmonitor.com/2006/0504/p16s01-legn.html.

Cristina Silva, *Some colleges crack down on laptop use in classroom: Teachers say it distracts from class participation*, BOSTON GLOBE, June 10, 2006, at B1, *available at* http://www. boston.com/news/local/articles/2006/06/10/some_college- s_crack_down.

Bruce Stewart, *Technology for blocking wireless signals spreads*, CNN.COM, Mar. 19, 2001, http://archives.cnn.com/2001/TECH/ industry/03/19/blocking.wireless.idg/.

Noam Cohen, *A Contributor to Wikipedia Has His Fictional Side*, N.Y. TIMES, Mar. 5, 2007, at C5.

Tracy L. McGaugh, *Laptops in the Classroom: Pondering the Possibilities*, 14 PERSP.: TEACHING LEGAL RESEARCH & WRITING 163 (2006).

Vivek Bhatnager, B-Schools in Second Life: It's more than just Fun and Games; It's the Confluence of Playing, Learning and Working, The Sloan Consortium (2008) *available at* http://www.sloanconsortium.org/viewarticle_SL

Paul L. Caron & Rafael Gely, *Taking Back the Law School Classroom: Using Technology to Foster Active Student Learning*, 54 J. LEGAL EDUC. 551 (2004).

Kristin B. Gerdy et al., *Expanding Our Classroom Walls: Enhancing Teaching and Learning through Technology*, 11 LEGAL WRITING 263 (2005).

Craig T. Smith, *Technology and Legal Education: Negotiating the Shoals of Technocentrism, Technophobia, and Indifference*, 1 J. ASS'N LEGAL WRITING DIRECTORS 247, (2001), *available at* http://www.alwd.org/publications/conference_publications.html.

Amy E. Sloan, Erasing Lines: Integrating the Law School Curriculum, 1 J. ASS'N LEGAL WRITING DIRECTORS 3 (2001), *available at* http://www.alwd.org/publications/conference_publications.html.

Chapter 8: The Future for Legal Education

Matthew M. Morrison, *Where Web 2.0 and Legal Information Intersect: Adjusting Course without Getting Lost* (Cornell Law Sch., Working Paper No. 35, 2008), *available at* http://lsr.nellco.org/cornell/clsops/papers/35/.

DONALD A. BLIGH, WHAT'S THE USE OF LECTURES? (2000).

J. Robert Brown Jr., *Blogs, Law School Rankings, and TheRacetotheBottom.org,* U. Denver Legal Studies Research Paper No. 07-33 (2007), http://ssrn.com/abstract=1003425.

Posting of Jeff T. Cobb to Mission to Learn: Learning. Technology. Change., *Five Themes for the Web 2.0 Learner,* http://blog.missiontolearn.com/2008/05/five-themes-for-the-web-20-learner/ (May 29, 2008).

Gene Koo, *New Skills, New Learning: Legal Education & the Promise of Technology* (Berkman Ctr. for Internet & Soc'y at Harvard Law Sch. Research Publication No. 2007-4, 2007).

EDWARD R. TUFTE, BEAUTIFUL EVIDENCE (2006).

Stephanie B. Goldberg, *Beyond the Socratic Method*, STUDENT LAW., Oct. 2007, at 18, *available at* http://www.abanet.org/lsd/studentlawyer/oct07/goldberg.shtml

Noam Cohen, *Now Professors Get Their Star Rankings, Too*, N.Y. TIMES, June 9, 2008, at C4.

DONALD L. FINKEL, TEACHING WITH YOUR MOUTH SHUT (2000).

Justin Appel, *Parents, teachers, kids speak up on ed tech*, E SCH. NEWS, Mar. 22, 2007, *available at* www.eschoolnews.com/news/showStory.cfm?ArticleID=6951.

Steve Lohr, *Publisher Tested the Waters Online, Then Dove In*, N.Y. TIMES, May 5, 2008, at C1, C6.

THINH NGUYEN, OPEN DOORS AND OPEN MINDS: WHAT FACULTY AUTHORS CAN DO TO ENSURE OPEN ACCESS TO THEIR WORK THROUGH THEIR INSTITUTION (April 2008) (a SPARC/Science Commons white paper).

Andrew Churches, *Bloom's Taxonomy Blooms Digitally*, TECHLEARNING, Apr. 1, 2008, http://www.techlearning.com/showArticle.php?articleID=196605124.

Law School Innovation, http://lsi.typepad.com/lsi/.

John Palfrey, *What is technology's role?*, NAT'L LAW J., Nov. 13, 2006, at 30.

Tovia Smith, *Singing Law Professor Rocks the Classroom*, N.P.R. MORNING EDITION, Nov. 14, 2007, *available at* http://www.npr.org/templates/story/story.php?storyID=16275927.

Tom Drummond, *A Brief Summary of the Best Practices in College Teaching: Intended to Challenge the Professional Development of All Teachers* (1995), *available at* http://www.fctel.uncc.edu/pedagogy/basicscoursedevelop/BestPractices.html.

Special Issue on Technology and Change in Educational Practice, 10 JOURNAL OF EDUC. TECH. & SOC'Y (Jan. 2007).

Cindy L. Lynch et al., *Table 1: Assumptions about Knowledge Related to Levels 1 Through 7 of the Reflective Judgment Model*, *in* Audrey A. Friedman, 89 ENGLISH J. 96, 98 (July 2000).

Anne H. Moore et al., *Active Learning and Technology: Designing Change for Faculty, Students, and Institutions*, EDUCAUSE, Sept./Oct. 2007, at 46.

John Seely Brown & Richard P. Adler, *Minds on Fire: Open Education, the Long Tail, and Learning 2.0*, EDUCAUSE, Jan./Feb. 2008, at 30.

ORI BRAFMAN & ROD A. BECKSTROM, THE STARFISH AND THE SPIDER: THE UNSTOPPABLE POWER OF LEADERLESS ORGANIZATIONS (2006).

Roberto L. Corrada, *A Simulation of Union Organizing in a Labor Law Class*, 46 J. LEGAL EDUC. 445 (1996).

MICHAEL HUNTER SCHWARTZ, EXPERT LEARNING FOR LAW STUDENTS (2d ed. 2008).

DONALD J. FINKEL, TEACHING WITH YOUR MOUTH SHUT (2000).

Daniel L. Barnett, *"Form Ever Follows Function": Using Technology To Improve Feedback on Student Writing in Law School*, 42 VAL. U. L. REV. 755 (2008).

Eli M. Noam, *WARNINGS: Electronics and the Future of Law Schools*, 17 J. CONTEMP. LEGAL ISSUES 51 (2008).

INDEX